IMAGINE ME

D0040599

BRENDA FANTROY-JOHNSON

This book is a work of non-fiction. Unless otherwise noted, the author and the publisher
make no explicit guarantees as to the accuracy of the information contained in this book
and in some cases, names of people and places have been altered to protect their privacy.

LifeRich Publishing is a registered trademark of The Reader's Digest Association, Inc.

LifeRich Publishing books may be ordered through booksellers or by contacting:

LifeRich Publishing
1663 Liberty Drive
Bloomington, IN 47403
www.liferichpublishing.com
1 (888) 238-8637

Because of the dynamic nature of the Internet, any web addresses or links contained in
this book may have changed since publication and may no longer be valid. The views
expressed in this work are solely those of the author and do not necessarily reflect the
views of the publisher, and the publisher hereby disclaims any responsibility for them.

Any people depicted in stock imagery provided by Thinkstock are models,
and such images are being used for illustrative purposes only.
Certain stock imagery © Thinkstock.

ISBN: 978-1-4897-1202-8 (sc)
ISBN: 978-1-4897-1203-5 (e)

Print information available on the last page.

LifeRich Publishing rev. date: 03/17/2017

For my brother Mike and all of the crabs still in the barrel

Where are we going?
It's not an issue of here or there.
And if you ever feel you can't
take another step imagine
how you might feel to arrive,
if not wiser, a little more aware
how to inhabit the middle ground
between misery and joy.
Trudge on. In the higher regions,
where the footing is unsure,
to trudge is to survive.

Stephen Dunn, Before We Leave

IMAGINE ME

Imagine me loving what I see
When the mirror looks at me
'Cause I, I imagine me

In a place of no insecurities
And I'm finally happy
'Cause I imagine me

Letting go of all of the ones who hurt me
'Cause they never did deserve me
Can You imagine me?

Saying no to thoughts that try to control me
Remembering all You told me
Lord, can You imagine me?

Over what my mamma said
And healed from what my daddy did
And I wanna live
And not read that page again

Imagine me
Being free, trusting You totally
Finally I can imagine me
I admit it was hard to see You being in love

With someone like me
Finally I can imagine me
Being strong and not letting people break me down
You won't get that joy this time around
Can You imagine me?

In a world where nobody has to live afraid Because of Your love, fear's gone away Can You imagine me?

Letting go of the past
And glad I have another chance
And my heart will dance
'Cause I don't have to read that page again

This song is dedicated to people like me.
Those that struggle with insecurities, acceptance, and even self-esteem.
You never felt good enough, you never felt pretty enough,
But imagine god whispering in your ear,
Letting you know that everything that has happened is now... Gone
It's gone, all gone
Every sin, every mistake, every failure

Depression? It's Gone
By faith. It's just gone

Low self-esteem? Hallelujah, it's gone
All gone

All my scars, all my pain, it's in the past. It's yesterday

All gone.

What your mother did. What your father did
It's gone, all gone

Kirk Franklin

CONTENTS

ACKNOWLEDGMENTS

I'd like to thank my mother who gave me the drive to continue by constantly telling me that if I stayed in school I would get out of the ghetto. She was right. Thank you Jennifer Wilhoit for believing that I could write this book, and my husband Harvey who taught me the value of learning how to nurture myself.

"The will of God is the ceaseless longing of the spirit in you to become all you're capable of being."
Pam Grout

PROLOGUE

A mong the well-to-do people all over the country, Bainbridge Island is known for its beauty. There are two great streets on Bainbridge. The first one is High School Road where, on a clear day, you can see the entire Olympic Mountains range. The other road, Miller, leads to a small retail district in the southern part of the island called Lynwood Center.

When I'm in my Mustang with the top down, driving down Miller Road, I feel as if I'm watching a movie and I'm the star. It's the film that begins with a car driving through a beautiful green forest. The sunlight filters and flickers through the trees. It's obviously warm, with a cool breeze, in this scene.

The wind blows through my hair. I smell pine trees. This is where I am, right in this moment. Serenity. Grace. Gratitude. Yes, I am at peace.

As I round the corner to come into Lynwood Center proper, I see Puget Sound. The scene opens up and, along the water, million-dollar houses appear from behind their hiding places. The skyline of Seattle is visible and Mt. Rainier is out to greet me. Just then I smell the mixed waters of the Sound. This saltwater/freshwater body is unique...just like me. I am here. I get to live on an island. Who would have thought?

And right then, I know. I have become just exactly what God knew I was capable of being.

When I heard my mama say: you've been slipping into darkness,
pretty soon you're gonna pay, War

HOW IN THE HELL DID THIS HAPPEN?

Once I drifted off from the pills and wine, I was in a very quiet place.

I am warm, comfortable, and content. I like it here and I want to stay. In the background, though, something is threatening this peace. I can just barely hear voices that gradually grow louder. I am upset by this. I hear a man say, "You have to talk louder to her. You have to wake her up." Then I hear voices that I know. "Brenda! Wake up!" they insist. I don't want to hear these voices. I don't want to wake up. Why does my family always have to ruin things? Just leave me alone and let me go. *But the familiar screaming voices are being encouraged by the strange man's voice. "She can hear you. Keep telling her to wake up." Finally, there is so much screaming that I cannot find my way back to the place inside where I can just be. Where it is quiet, serene, and safe.*

"Shut the fuck up. I hear you!" Those were my first words out of the coma. Of course, I did not know that I had been in a coma for almost two weeks. I've always said that this was the most peace I've ever felt. But then I am awake and I realize that I'm alive. I cry because I don't want to be alive.

Why the fuck am I still here? Of all of the times to be concerned, to act as if he cared. I found out that Thomas woke up in the middle of the night and saw that something was wrong. I'm not sure what tipped him off or even why he woke up. For him to call 911 was so out of character, so un-Thomas-like. That's the one thing I did not plan on. He was supposed to get up early and either find me dead or ignore me like he always did and take off in search of that morning's blow. Instead,

1

there I was alive, waking up in a large, stark white hospital room with huge windows. A doctor I did not know was standing over me. My sister Deborah, and my brother, Mike, were there too. I was not happy to see them. I was not happy to see anyone.

I knew what was coming next, the question without an answer: Why?

I once heard someone say, when asked why he tried to kill himself, "If you have to ask, then you would never understand." This is exactly how I felt. I wanted to *not live* more than I wanted to live. I decided to opt out of life. I was 20 years old. I had enough of this life and was ready for whatever came next. I really can't blame this feeling on any particular thing; it was a combination of many things. I felt like I did not have a stake in the world. I felt like I had gotten off on the wrong foot and I had botched up my life.

Deep down inside I was just tired. Tired of the beatings Thomas gave me just because he could. Tired of the endless search for money to buy food, drugs, diapers. Tired of the things I had to do just to maintain some semblance of a life. I can't blame my alcoholism for this suicide attempt. Life was just not all it was cracked up to be. I figured death would be easier.

My daughter, Tamiko, was learning to stand up but was not yet walking and I felt passionate about giving her a shot at a better life, a life without me. At the time, I really felt that this was the best thing for her. Because she had not yet been diagnosed with sickle cell anemia, I did not know that she would face her own battle her entire life. She would need me there to help her fight it.

I was very sore. Sore all over. I ignored all of their questions, trying to find my peaceful place again. But there was no more peace to be had for a very long time. The thing about suicide is that when you try to do it the way I did, by mixing muscle relaxers and alcohol, there are bound to be some side effects. I was awake but not lucid. When I would come-to I saw things. I would open my eyes to large monster-sized spiders crawling on the ceiling. I woke up rattled by my own blood-curdling screams. The nurses would rush in to assure me that I was okay. They made sure I had my call button so that when I saw a tiny bug slowly swallow a very large one, I could push my button and they would come to my rescue. This was not worth living through. I cried continually. I'm not sure why I'm here. I don't want to be here.

Of course, I never answered any questions about it. I made sure that everyone knew it was probably an accident. I was smart enough to see the pattern, the way they sent social workers and psychiatrists to talk to me. I could see where this was going. I was not crazy, or maybe I was. But I did not want to be locked up anywhere. They asked questions about my frame of mind when I took the pills. Was I depressed? Yes, but I was not going to tell them that. I was not going to be a textbook-crazy-loony-tune. *It was a mistake. I had back and shoulder pain. I took the pills, lost track of how many (thirty), and had a few drinks with my boyfriend. I screwed up that chance and now here come the consequences. No, I don't need any help. Thanks for saving my life (not!).*

It took about two weeks for me to come down from the high. I also had to convince everybody that it was safe to allow me out into the same cruel world that I tried to escape from. All was lost. My one chance to opt-out was foiled by a heroin addict who beat me for no reason.

Thomas was not at the apartment when my sister brought me home. After she left I held my daughter tight and cried. I tried to explain to her that I was so sorry for screwing up the suicide. I really believed that now she would get cheated out of a good life because she was stuck with me as a mother. What a selfish bitch I was. She may have been the only solid, good thing in my life. At the time, I did not see it. I only saw how I was going to screw things up. I decided that I must be here for something. God must have kept me here for something. I wish he had asked me first. Why don't we have a choice? Where was the free will bullshit I had heard about?

So my life continued. The fights and the beatings continued. After a few days I had to go back to the clinic for a follow-up from the hospital stay.

The appointment was to get the dialysis tube out of my ankle and to look at the other incisions to be sure I was healing. The suicide attempt had taken a toll on me and apparently my kidneys had failed. The doctor had not wanted to discharge me from the hospital. But because it was Christmas, I appealed to his kindness. "How would it be for my daughter to go through this holiday without her mother?" This is ironic because I had no qualms about leaving her for the rest of her life. So I was discharged with the tube in my foot.

The clinic was in a small neighborhood not far from where I had once lived after the riots when I was a child. I stood outside of the doctor's office, looking around and remembering when the Detroit Tigers won the World Series in 1968; I was ten years old and my siblings and I broke my mother's rules so we could celebrate in the streets not far from here. I walked into the tiny, crowded office to register with the woman behind the bulletproof glass. I wondered whether this was a real doctor or just another pill doctor.

A cloud of smoke hovered in the room from folks puffin' on their cigarettes. I got an intense lump in my throat from the smoke, so I asked the receptionist for a cup of water. I began coughing and my throat felt scratchy and tight.

I go into an intense coughing fit and can't get the water down because I can't stop coughing. People are looking at me as I try to convey the panic by pointing at my throat. I can't breathe. I feel as if there is a vice grip around my windpipe. People are starting to see me panic. They shout to the receptionist to call 911. She is hesitant but then she calls. Someone helps me outside where I'm trying to understand. I'm not getting any air and this is going to kill me. It's unlike anything I've ever experienced. People are crowding around me and they see that this is a life or death situation. They help me back into the doctor's office. The lady behind the bulletproof glass says they are not allowed to treat me and that the paramedics cannot pick me up inside the clinic. Well, ain't that a bitch. I'm going to die outside a doctor's office. They don't have oxygen in this place? That confirms that this is not a real doctor. I still can't breathe outside. I lie down on the sidewalk wheezing. I hear sirens. "Hold on Brenda," I tell myself as I hear them get closer.

They arrive and I'm questioned like I am a dope fiend. What did I take? What am I on? I can't talk. I've got a hot poker down my throat. Feels like a balloon that has been tied in a knot, only a snippet of air getting through. I'm gonna die. Funny, now I don't want to die. I pass out. I wake up on a gurney being wheeled into a large operating room. I have an oxygen mask on my face which is somehow making it harder to breathe. Of course, there are papers to sign. I do this quickly, without looking. On my chest is an x-ray of my neck, and a foreign doctor I can barely understand points to a huge dark spot that is blocking my airway. My windpipe is damaged. I'm suffocating. He's telling me what he's going to try. Do I give him permission? I scream with my eyes, "Yes, please do whatever you have to do!"

What a far cry from opting out of life. Now I am fighting to live! I want the doctor to fight for me, too.

When I woke up, I knew right away that life as I knew it had changed. My chin was tight and I could not lift my head up. My chest felt like an elephant with spikes was sitting on me and I was dizzy and sore all over.

I could not speak. The doctor came in to give me some of the details about my emergency surgery. They removed one inch of my infected windpipe. I took what felt like a deep breath which caused a great deal of pain. I was given a cup with a straw. This was equally painful. The water magnified the pain as it went down. My hand reached for the obstruction that was holding my head down. The doctor explained that my chin was stitched to the top of my chest. There was an incision from my throat down to the top of my belly with two holes in it so that the incision could drain. I felt like I was the freak in a horror show. I asked for a mirror but was not really prepared for what I saw. I looked hideous. I was split down the middle, bruised, and had more than twelve staples running down my chest. I could see a cloudy liquid oozing out of a small hole at the bottom of the incision. I was quite calm about the entire thing. I was alive and I could breathe. It hurt like hell but when I weighed what it felt like before, I was ahead of the game.

Still, I began to develop shame around the entire ordeal. I wore two hospital gowns to hide the scar. My hospital room had no windows and I kept it dark. There was a TV hanging from the ceiling and I would listen to it because I could not see it. There was an odor from the drainage that was collecting in the mostly-sealed space between my chin and my neck. I was not able to shower or get out of bed for days. The nurses gave me sponge baths and I complained about the smell of my neck. One nurse devised a way to clean this area using a dampened swab. I was ashamed that the nurse saw how nasty it was in the crevice. I only let her clean this once before I took over.

I remember my friend Bennie coming to see me while I was in the hospital. I would try to laugh when he walked in. Because of my head being sewn to my chest, the only way I could tell who people were was by identifying their feet. Bennie had big feet, so I could tell it was him as soon as he walked in. Bennie and I would walk to the smoking area. Hole in my throat, chest cut open and cracked like a crab, and I still smoked. I know I was quite a sight walking around all sewn down, clutching my gown so no one could see my shame. Thomas may have come to see me once. First time he saw my scar down my chest he said, "Damn! You look like Frankenstein." He laughed. I cried after he left because he was so right.

I stayed in the hospital for quite a long time, before they finally removed the stitches from my chin to my chest. I was left with scars on both sides of my chin and no way to hide them. I also had no way to deal with what had happened to me. I was not offered a psychiatrist to talk to. I was expected to just go on living, twenty years old and scarred for life. Over the years, doctors have asked me why I was cut all the way from my neck down to my belly just to operate on my throat. But I held no animosity toward the doctor who made that cut. I was just thankful that he read the pleading look in my eyes and did what he had to do to save my life. It was up to me to deal with what I looked like. I could breathe and that was what mattered. How did I get to this place?

My relationship with Thomas started out great. I was sixteen or seventeen years old when Barbara, my neighbor, asked me to babysit. The story was that she was "well-off." She worked for Chrysler and may have had other questionable income. When she came to my door she seemed very nice. I said, "Sure, I can babysit." So we went up the block to her house. She showed me around and showed me this beautiful black baby doll of a baby: curly hair and big, beautiful eyes. Barbara showed me how to change and feed her. Then she left. I put the baby to sleep and cautiously checked out her very nice house. "Well-off" by ghetto standards.

Then Thomas came looking for Barbara. He was fine! Coffee colored skin and nice afro, lean and tall. I guess I was taken right away. I told him that Barbara was not home and that the baby was asleep so he should probably come back later. He questioned me about who I was and where I lived. He flirted with me and tried to kiss me. I was blown away. The next thing I knew we were getting busy, kissing and rolling on the bed. Just then I heard the door and we were nearly caught by Barbara. That's when I found out they were boyfriend / girlfriend and that she was giving him money for drugs. Thomas was a con man, a charmer, and a wolf in sheep's clothing. He was just the right amount of bad. I fell in love with him. He would come over when I babysat and we snuck around while Barbara was at work.

One day I heard that Barbara found out about Thomas and me, that she was going to kick my ass, so I hid out at home. After spending the day alone at home peeping out of the windows in fear, Barbara showed up. She banged on the door. As I peeked out the curtain, Barbara asked, "You been sleeping with my man?" She was a hefty woman and intimidated me from the first day I met her. "No," I said. "I want you to stay away from Thomas, and don't even bother to come back down to my house. If I see your face I'm gonna kick your skinny ass." That ended my babysitting career but increased my desire for bad boys. Of course we continued to see each other and—though I didn't know it—Thomas also continued seeing Barbara whenever he needed money for drugs. There was a progression of other women, too.

My brother and I were just coming to the realization that our father was not coming back home. I was reaching out for structure in the only way I knew how. Crazy as it seemed, Thomas and his family provided that structure.

Thomas had two brothers and five sisters (from a number of different daddies) who, at one time or another, lived at his mother's house. All or most of them had babies running around, and all of this was headed-up by Dorothy, the mother. Their house was across the street from where my brother and I lived, and it was always nasty. There were always roaches and piles of dishes in the kitchen sink. Every once in a while, Thomas' sister Yvette and I would do a major clean up and cook. It consisted of piling the dishes on the table, removing all the roaches, washing the dishes, and frying three or four chickens for the whole clan. I wanted to keep the place clean, but Yvette and I were the only ones who ever noticed. The babies walked around with filthy diapers that were always full. They had black feet from walking barefoot on the floors. You could not sit your beer or pop can down, let alone any food, because that was fair game for roaches. Sleeping or sitting always involved casually brushing off crawlers. This was normal.

The day of the suicide attempt was a typical day—"typical" in the sense that I woke up and began to muddle through the day. These were the mornings when I would question my existence. Did I really want to go through another day of the same old thing? I dressed and fed my fifteen-month old daughter, Tamiko. Thomas came in from selling the pills and we followed our normal routine.

That morning I went to the doctor to get my prescription for muscle relaxers. I remember the crowded waiting rooms. People milling around. The whole place was a sham. We all knew why we were there: to get prescription pills to sell. No one there was really sick. Sick people went to real doctors. I checked in at the front window, giving the nurse my Medicaid insurance information. Then I went outside for a smoke. People were walking around talking about the usual things: who was a good source to sell pills to, who had gotten caught, which doctor gave the most pills, who was giving the best price for the pills. Of course, these details were left to Thomas; my job was to simply get the pills.

I answered the questions that the doctor asked. These were just a ruse to make it seem as if he really was treating me for back pain. I could have started singing the blues and I believe they still would have given me a prescription for the muscle relaxers. The doctor was receiving money from Medicaid so any answer would have worked. Stopping around the corner at the pharmacy, I got the pills.

I made the decision that it was time. I had thought about it before but was always too chicken to try. I always talked myself out of it. But not this time. Back at home, I put my baby to bed and walked out into the night. I often put Tamiko to bed and left the house, not thinking that I had any other options. She would sleep through until we got back. But this would be another thing that I would later add to the list of items to make restitution for, that deepened the layers of guilt and shame about being an unfit mother.

Walking I had a clear thought. The act itself did not feel premeditated but I felt like I had prepared for this event for the last five years of my life. It all seemed to line up. I knew what I was going do and how to do it. The plan was there in my head like it belonged, like it was right. I reasoned that by removing myself from her life, Tamiko would have a better chance. We walked several blocks to the beer store and bought two fifths of red Wild Irish Rose wine. This was our usual. Even though I disliked the taste, I could count on it to do the job. I thought all the way home. I knew that this time would be the last time. The only person I would miss was my daughter. But I knew my sister would take care of her.

When we got home with the booze and Thomas was not looking, I took the muscle relaxers that I had left. I sat with him and proceeded to drink my bottle of Rose. He did not seem to notice any difference when I went to bed that night. I remember thinking that finally I would get some peace. That's all I really wanted. I was not enjoying this life. I wanted to opt out. Maybe see what the afterlife was about. It had to be better than this.

THE GOOD CHILD

T he earliest memory I have is from when I was three years old. My family was living in a downstairs apartment on Seward Street on the west side of Detroit. Our neighborhood was nice. I did not know that then, but location is very important to my story.

I'm a very small child and our family is happy and excited! We've had one of the largest snowfalls in the history of Detroit. My mother, Lillie May Jones; my brothers, George and Mike; and my sister, Deborah, were all standing at the walkout patio door looking out. They were amazed that the snow covered the entire height of the door. We were snowed in! That meant we got to stay in. I was not old enough for school but I was happy because everybody else was happy. We played inside and eventually the snow melted enough and neighbors came to dig us out. This was when the city was its cleanest, all white and pretty. Usually, it was difficult or impossible for traffic to move until the streets got plowed. Every neighborhood I've ever lived in seemed to be last on the plow list.

We lived in this downstairs flat for just a short time. Yet my few memories of this apartment are very clear. For example, until I grew too big, my first bed was a drawer in a large dresser. This would become one of many stories about me that I love: "Yep. As a baby I slept in a dresser drawer."

Deborah and George were my oldest two siblings; George was named after my father, so we simply called him "Jr." Though still dark, they were lighter-skinned. It's amazing how two or three skin shades could make such a difference. Most folks don't realize the subtleness of race, but all Black people know these differences. Mike, my third eldest sibling, was dark-skinned like me. We shared a bond—being the last two born, and being the not so good-looking children. We also both bore nicknames that had "black" in them. Mike got the worst of this.

Other more difficult memories from this early apartment involve my father who lived elsewhere, and my mother who slept in a twin bed in a small, doorless room of our apartment. I remember my father busting in the front door one night. The fight that followed began to shape my image of my father. He burst through the door, tall, drunk, and angry. My mother didn't say much, but my father was going on about her behavior. Apparently she had gone down to a neighborhood bar and confronted my dad as he was partying with another woman. She had, in his words, "showed her ass." Before my mother could get out her retort, he had slapped her. He began punching her and pushing her into walls. The four of us children were crying, pleading for him to stop. I thought I could help. So as he bent down to kick my mother on the floor, I jumped on his back. The other kids were kicking him and screaming for him to leave our mother alone. The next thing I knew, he stood up with me on his back and shook me off. I flew through the air. My back hit the wall and the impact knocked the air out of me. He stopped, looked around at the carnage, and stormed out. I did not understand this violence. My mom was only five feet tall and there's no way she could defend herself from my dad.

Over the next few years I came to understand that my mom deeply loved my dad. This love was powerful and deep. It would shape the rest of her life and ours. It was a strange time. The four of us, and my mother: striving together. Even though they had three previous children together, my dad had not married my mom until after I was born. I like to say that I'm the one that made the other kids legitimate. Though he always lived nearby, we never lived together as a family.

Being a single parent of four was hard on my mom. She would leave nights to go to work, leaving the older kids in charge. My mom was a hard worker. When I asked what her job was, she told me, "I clean houses for white folks." She would sometimes need to take me with her to work. She would say to me, "Brenda, be nice and don't touch nothing; I can't afford to replace anything there." These folks lived in big houses. I would follow behind her trying to stay out of the way. This was a good job and nobody thought that it was demeaning in any way. It supplemented the welfare money we were getting.

I had a huge attachment to my mom. When she would have to leave me at home, I would sit on the couch and rock back and forth, bumping the back of my head softly on the couch. I came up with a song. Thumb in mouth, I would sing: "I want my ma-mah, my ma-mah, my ma- ma-ma-mah." I often did this for hours. My older sister used to say, "You are gonna bump all your hair out." Deborah used to comb my hair and she was right, eventually my hair fell out and refused to grow.

My father worked for Great Lakes Steel Company. This was a great job for him and a rarity for a black man. When I was older, he shared stories about racism on the job. He also shared other stories that would shock us, making us laugh. He had a great sense of humor, was very loud and animated. I loved him as much as my mother did. I never witnessed another physical fight between them, but there were other shouting matches. He would breeze through every so often handing out nickels and quarters to me and my younger brother; the older kids did not want to take the money out of loyalty to my mom. They had seen and experienced more life with Daddy than I had. Because my mother loved him hard, so did I.

Most of my time alone was spent reading, or outdoors discovering the neighborhood. When I got bored, I would go down the block to a very pretty house. There was an old woman who lived there. She had a wonderfully small house on a large parcel of land. She was an avid gardener who had all types of very fragrant flowers. I would stand outside of her fence looking at all of the flowers, smelling all of the sweetness. If she was home, she would let me inside the fenced area for a closer look. Sometimes I would just lie back in the grass with my eyes closed and smell the roses and other flowers.

It is there that I began my habit of daydreaming about what my life would be like when I grew up. I would lie there, and in those moments I was in charge of what my future looked like. I would have a nice husband, good-looking and kind. I would have two children, a sweet boy and a girl. I would live in a modest house, not too big or too small. I would work in a job helping kids, maybe as a teacher. These daydreams continued throughout my life. There were times when this woman would have to shake me out of my thoughts because I had been there so long.

This was a happy time in my life. We spent a lot of time playing. We played board games like Operation or Clue when it would rain or was too late to go outside. We had a great time saying things like "Mrs. Pee Cock." Both words just filled us with laughter. Other times in the evenings we would all gather around the black and white TV to watch my Mom's favorite shows like "The Fugitive" and "Ironside." There was always music, food, and laughter in my childhood home. We lived around the corner from Hitsville USA. This was where Motown had its recording studio. This was a time when everyone you met claimed to be a cousin of Smokey Robinson or Diana Ross. Music was everywhere. I was happy and I really believed everyone else was happy too. We would listen to all of the Motown music that was prevalent at that time.

I think that my mom felt they were speaking to her when Diana Ross and the Supremes sang hits like "I Hear a Symphony," "You Can't Hurry Love," "My World Is Empty Without You," and other soulful songs about lost love. She pined away for my father—a man who lived just around the corner with another woman, who left my mom with four little children. What that must have felt like, I don't know. She never said anything bad or mean about my father. My mom was a proud woman and the story was that she would never divorce my dad because she was Catholic. But apart from the label, she never practiced this religion. I believe she always hoped he would come back to her.

I tried to make my mom happy by being The Good Child. I would behave like the white kids on TV. I even tried to talk "proper" like they did. My brothers and sister would make fun of me for this, especially the way that I pronounced certain words. For example, at the dinner table I would say, "Please pass the Bu-tter." That would crack everyone up.

I was the entertainer. I would dance for my mom and she loved it. Whenever she had friends over for a night of fast-paced card games of Bid Whist or poker, where she'd get a cut of each game for hosting the party, she would call me to the middle of the floor. "Dance, Baby," she would say. And I would, as they said in those days, "cut a rug." With mama and the friends' encouragement and with the sounds of the music I would feel like a star. My personality was developing: I tried to be the family clown.

I also had a bit of entrepreneurialism in me at an early age. I made small change by exploiting the laziness of my sisters and brothers. I would see what chores they did not want to do and offer to do them for a price. Dishes were fifty cents; laundry was five cents for socks, ten cents for pants. I made most of my money from my brothers. Though I did a lot of dishes for my sister.

For some reason I was chosen from the four of us kids to go on weekend visits with my dad and his live in girlfriend who we knew as "Ms. Mary." I never thought it was strange that my dad lived around the corner from us. I knew he and my mom were married. I knew Mom loved him and I knew he lived with Ms. Mary. I felt special and unique to be the "chosen" child who got to do this. I did not know at the time that the others did not want to go.

My dad was well known in the neighborhood as "Nigga George." Other black folks said this with respect. He had gained this respect by being able to land a job at the steel company and being promoted to a crane operator position. This was a big deal for a black man. Maybe success went to his head, I don't know. I do know that at the time I was proud to have him as my daddy.

Daddy would visit us on Christmas and sometimes bring things. I don't ever remember thinking we were poor. I had clothes and toys. Most of these clothes came from both the five and dime store or from out of a Goodfellow Box. I remember this one time when he walked in the door with a bike. It was used but was in good condition. I was so happy. Mama kept pressuring him to tell her where he had got the bike. He said it was not stolen, if that's what she thought. I loved that bike.

I learned how to ride the bike with my sister holding me up and holding the back of the bike while running behind me as I pedaled. She would let me go as I got to a house down the street that had a chain link fence in front. I would ride unassisted for twenty feet, just enough to feel like I was flying, then I would bang into the side of the fence to stop myself. I got all banged up, but those few feet felt like I was a bird flying free. Then I learned how to ride without help! Although, I was not allowed to go too far, or go in the street, riding my bike allowed me a way to be alone and free all at the same time.

Seward was where I learned how to be in the world. I was the baby of the family and it was hard always following what the others did. My place in the family was established slowly, and then it was entrenched as if it had always been that way. Mama gave me special favor, not to the point of me being spoiled, but enough that I always felt special and unique. I could look at her and tell that she loved me more and I bet the other kids felt the same way. We often joked with each other about which one of us mom loved the most. When we asked her, she always said the same thing: she loved us all equally.

I began to secretly accept that I was different. I believed that I should be my own person. I always thought of myself as special. Though I did not know why, deep in my soul I knew big things were going to happen to me.

My Mom's staunch rule was that we had to stay on the block unless she gave permission, and we had to be home by the time that the streetlights came on. We didn't live far from the General Motors headquarters on Woodward Avenue. My mom would let us walk there on weekends. There was a movie theater and one of the first of its kind, hamburger fast food places. We would see a movie and then get a burger. We felt very grown up. Other times we would go to the GM building and run and play in the several block long underground tunnel. This was always fun. We would scream and listen to the echo reverberate off the walls. Sometimes we would get chased by the security guard, and we could always outrun him.

There would even be times when my mom would take us to the show. We said we didn't like that too much. But I really loved it. My mom had a habit of talking back to the movie screen, especially if she'd had a few beers. "Don't go in there," she would shout. Folks would look at us. "No, run. Don't fall." People would then shush us. Sometimes it was hilarious. Mama was full of fire; she didn't take no mess from anyone.

This was a great time to be a kid. We were allowed to ride the bus together or alone. I loved to go downtown to walk amongst the big Detroit buildings. I would go to the Kresge store or the Sanders store and have soda and ice cream. At Christmas time, we would ride over in my mother's boyfriend's car to Grosse Point Park, an affluent area along the Detroit River. We would gawk at the elaborate Christmas lights and I would add to my dreams of what my adult life would look like to include living in a house by the water.

There was another neighborhood that we heard about too, a place called "Hastings Street." The story is that my dad was born and raised there. This area was fondly known as "Black Bottom." Only the hardest criminals and gangs lived there. My dad claimed that he was lucky to get out of that neighborhood alive. I thought that the people in my neighborhood lived there because they wanted to. I never imagined people lived someplace because of economic conditions. We never worried too much about crime, or about kids being snatched or molested. I really liked our neighborhood. It was safe and folks were friendly. This period of my life seemed to have lasted forever, but it was really only two or three years that are so vivid with fun childhood memories.

SCHOOL DAYS

G oodfellow boxes were given to poor kids to make sure every kid got something for Christmas. The boxes all had the same types of things in them: two shirts, a pair of pants, underwear, socks, and hard candy. The girls also got a White baby doll. After Christmas vacation when we all went back to school, you could tell who the Goodfellow kids were because they all had on the same plaid shirts. The thing we liked the most was the hard candy that was shaped like Christmas—green trees and white boxes with red ribbons.

Mama had to sign us up for this through the Detroit Public Schools. The school also was where we signed up and were treated for dental care and immunizations. We also received some assistance from the State. This was during the time when social workers visited the home and did walk-throughs looking for signs of a man living on the premises. Fathers weren't allowed in the home and was a reason to stop any assistance. I felt strange when these visits occurred. I felt like it was not right, but that there was nothing I could do about it. These visits made my mother agitated and worried. Even though we knew there was not a man in our home, we were all afraid the worker would find something out of order and the benefits would stop.

My life was full of wonder and exploration, it seemed that everything was new. I spent an enormous amount of time alone either in thought or reading. I was a bookworm at an early age. I loved to get deep inside a book; fairy tales were the best. I discovered getting good grades made my mother happy and it was another way to stick out, to be special or unique from the other kids. It was not easy because all of us got good grades.

My first day of school was very eventful. Our block was short and all of the neighbors seemed to know us. Mama, my brothers and sister, and I walked to school together that first day of kindergarten, I was so excited to go even though it meant being away from Mama and the specialness we shared. Now it was my turn to see what this school thing was all about.

Even at an early age I knew that school would not be a problem for me academically. I could already read a little bit and knew my numbers. There were gauges to my intelligence that were measured by my brothers and sisters before me. The age we first crawled or walked, when we first said "mama," who knew their ABC's, and so on. It seemed like I ranked in the top two.

So on my first day of school we were walking up the block and the only thing I was really worried about was crossing the bridge over the Lodge freeway to get to the school on the other side. I was okay when someone was holding my hand, but my mind had already begun to think about when I would have to do this alone. We got to the bridge and the four-lane freeway below was loud with traffic zipping by. It roared whenever an 18-wheeler truck zoomed by and the whole bridge shook from the vibration. I held Mama's hand tighter and really tried not to think about it.

My first love was my Kindergarten teacher. More specifically, I fell in love with the nylons on her legs. She would sit in one of those child-sized wooden chairs and read to us. We would form a circle around her and I was always right in front, next to those long, silky legs. I would stare at them and finally I got up the nerve one day to touch them as we sat there. It was more like stroking them. I had never seen or felt nylon stockings before. This was the softest, most pleasurable material I had ever felt. Everyday I could not wait until it was story time. I would run to the front and wait until she got engrossed into the story and then run my hand along those wonderful soft, long sticks! There was nothing erotic about it; I just loved the feel. Eventually a note was sent home and that put a stop to my stocking fun. Even to this day I love to feel my legs in a nice pair of nylons. I feel dressed up and adult-like.

My second love was Hat, though his real name was Curtis. He always wore a cap on his head, whether it was summer or winter. It was the kind with the flaps over the ears styled after a leather aviator pilot cap. I never thought anything of it. In fact, I liked him in his cap. The color of his skin was caramel brown and he was a bit taller than I was. I thought he was really something! He would walk on the other side of the street when I would walk home from school. We would steal glances at each other across the street. I knew he liked me, and he knew that I liked him. Eventually he crossed the street and walked me home. I think on the second or third time we finally spoke to each other. Do you like me? Can I be your boyfriend? This was high- level conversation for a nine-year-old.

I made the mistake of telling my sister, actually gushing to her, so happy that I had an admirer. One weekend morning, Curtis decided to pay me a surprise visit. When he knocked on the door I still had nightclothes on and my hair was all over my head. When my sister told me who was at the door, I ran and hid in a closet. I could not let him see me like that. My sister, Deborah, dragged me out of the closet and, while my older brothers grilled this poor ten-year-old boy, my sister quickly braided my hair while I put on some appropriate clothing. Deborah rushed me back out to the front, where I immediately got a case of the tongue-tieds and shyness. Eventually, we made our way outside and sat on the front porch. This was a date, my very first date. After that, we held hands on the way home from school. We were officially "girlfriend and boyfriend."

One day Curtis was walking down the street wearing his aviator cap and my oldest brother, Jr., shouted, "Look Brenda, your boyfriend "Hat" is outside." This statement seemed to crack everyone up; they laughed and teased me mercilessly. I looked out of the window and I could tell that not only had Curtis heard the uproar, but he felt that I was making fun of him too. I was too embarrassed to correct this or to even talk to him about it. Curtis was one of the good guys.

BOB-LO

W e used to go on trips as a family. Not big vacations, but from my child's eyes they were magnificent. Detroit had a huge boat that would go to Bob-Lo Island Amusement Park. We would get dressed up in our best summer outfits to get on the bus and head downtown to the Bob-Lo boat dock! Just the name evoked fun and happiness. Black and white folks alike loved this place.

The boat had food and music. Usually a band or DJ would play oldies and new stuff. Kids and old folks would get in the middle of the very large dance floor and "cut a rug." There were a lot of hot dogs and popcorn. Most folks brought coolers with pop and beer. The boat took about an hour to get to the island. I always thought we were something! Not everyone could afford to go to Bob-Lo. Though I don't think it was very expensive, it had to have cost a pretty penny for us to do that with four kids in our family. But every summer we would go at least once.

We would dance 'til we were exhausted then we would sit in the white deck chairs that were situated around the edges of the boat. We would enjoy the Detroit River, watching Canada pass by on one side and Detroit on the other. This was very peaceful. I loved the water and the smells of the river and fresh air. My mother enjoyed the ride also.

The excitement would build as we made our way along the river. Then Bob-Lo Island would come into view. It was spectacular, with green grass and pretty flowers hosting all kinds of amusement rides. You could see the huge roller coaster that ran the length of the left side of the island. The words "Welcome to Bob-Lo Island" were spelled out on a raised hill with red and white flowers. There was music and so many rides it was hard what to choose to do first.

We would pile off the boat and lug our stuff to the picnic area to establish a base. My mother would stake out a table and lay out the rules. We were to periodically check in with her. She would have her small cooler of Black Label beer and maybe a bottle of wine. We would make a plan of action and, after a few squabbles, off we would go. What fun and freedom! I would wander around the island, knowing this place like the back of my hand, going on all of my favorite rides. The Tilt-a-Wheel, bumper cars, and Scary House were among my favorites, and even Mama got on the train that would go from one side of the island to the other side. Then we would all meet at our picnic spot for sandwiches, potato chips, watermelon, and pop.

Late in the afternoon, we would congregate to pack up our stuff. We always wanted to be sure not to miss the last boat. I never knew what would happen if someone missed it, but my imagination told me that it would be very, very bad. Rumor had it that people who had missed the last boat were somehow found dead the next morning, as if Bob-Lo was all fun during the day but scary killer clowns came out at night. There had also been rumors of bodies being found of the folks who got left behind, or who stayed intentionally just to see what would happen.

The trip home on the boat was always the same. I always thought of the rides I did not get to and we would vow to do it differently next time. The energy on the return trip was much more somber. Babies and kids were tired and sleepy, parents had less energy and patience. Even the DJ or band would play somber music. It was as if all of the reality of life was pushing in and pushing out all of the fantasy and excitement of the day. Of course, alcohol played a part in this too. The adults were drunk. Our return trip always included my mother standing against the railing watching the boat cut through the river water. Looking sad, and being a bit blitzed, she would always say the same thing about how the water was calling her. How she might be better off jumping in the water so it would pull her down. This was very scary to me. I always hated the return trip because my mother was always depressed. I always felt that if I held her hand everything would be alright. I would plead with her not to jump.

At some point in all of our trips to the island with my mother, I got used to her talk and I would just listen because I felt she needed someone to do that. In the end, I know that even if she wanted to jump she would not have. I only came to that conclusion because experience taught me. But even then there was a glimmer in the back of my mind of "what if" and so I would stand there holding her hand, listening to her talk about the cold, deep, blue Detroit River and how it was calling her.

There were other times, too, that my mom would get sad and talk about dying. Mama used to tell us in a very serious tone, "I'm not gonna be here all of your life kids; one day I'm gonna die." How I hated these talks. She would gather us together and try to explain about this hole that was in her heart that would probably kill her. Between the sobs and tears of us children, she would make us promise to stay in school and to be good and focused. Because, as she put it, "it's the only way out." I don't want you all to end up like me with only a high school education. She told us more than once that her death was coming soon. There was nothing that the doctors could do. I didn't believe her. This was just another story she needed for me to hear. So I listened and cried.

When we lived on Marcus Street, my mama would take me to the store with her sometimes during the day. We would head out through the alley behind our house. We picked up any bottles we found to cash in at the store. This was quality time. Precious time spent with my mama. When we got to the store she would buy a bottle of Mogen David Concord Red wine. If there was enough money left over, I would be able to get some candy or gum. I especially liked the candy necklaces which I would eat all the way home. Mama would also buy a pack of Pall Mall cigarettes without the filters. She would smoke these and constantly need to spit out the tobacco that would cling to her tongue and lips. Sometimes at home she would ask me to light her cigarette from the stove in the kitchen, and I would mimic her spitting out the tobacco.

We made our trips through the alley instead of down the street. I thought we did that so we could pick up bottles, but it was really so that the neighbors did not see us going to the beer and wine store every day. My mom would occasionally visit the neighborhood bar around the corner from our house. Though kids were not allowed in, if I was with my mom and it was day time, the bartender would let me in for the few minutes it took my mom to drink a shot of whiskey.

I spent a lot of time with my mama. I liked to watch TV with her, watch her cooking in the kitchen, or talking to the neighbors. My mama's nickname was Lil, short for Lillie Mae, and some of our neighbors called me Little Lil.

RIOTS

When we heard the news about President Kennedy's assassination I thought my mom was going to faint. She started crying and screaming, "Oh Lord, they killed the president." I did not understand why this affected her so much but she cried and cried. I cried too. I did not like the way she and the rest of our neighbors felt and acted. I could feel in my gut that something was coming. Times were changing and not for the better.

I started to see things a bit different after President Kennedy was shot. It was like my eyes got a bit clearer about our situation and position in life. I saw my neighborhood in a different way. There were a lot of Black people here, in all walks of life. Men in sharkskin suits with flamboyant hats on, walking to a musical beat of their own. I somehow knew or heard about 12th Street, where pimps and "hoes" made their living at night. Twelfth Street was like the ghetto downtown. People only went there during the day to shop or go to the cleaners. At nighttime, it was the place to go to for sordid activities.

July 23, 1967 started like any other day. My father had come over in the darkness of the morning to pick up my oldest brother George to go fishing somewhere on the Detroit River. Fishing always had to start at some ungodly early hour. This was one of my father's favorite pastimes. I was too young to go and my sister did not want to go. As the oldest, George Jr. was my father's favorite child, and so my father was always trying to win him over.

When the rest of us woke up, we went about our weekend day as normal. I was sitting on the front porch enjoying a solitary game of throw-ball-jacks, when I heard Mama screaming and crying. "Oh Lord, now they have shot Dr. King! What are we gonna do now?" She cried for a long time. When she stopped, the grief on her face and in her voice was replaced with fear.

I had never seen this look before. My mama was not afraid of anything. I had seen her many times take on men much bigger than she was and talk them into docile puppies. But this expression scared me. So I started crying, knowing that if it scared Mama, it was very bad.

Mama came out of the house. Her face was distorted with worry. "Where are your sister and brother?" Deborah was not far and came when called, but Mike and Jr. were gone. I noticed an electricity in the air and all of a sudden people were out of their houses, running through the streets. There was whooping and hollering, and they carried all kinds of things: TVs, lamps, record players, clothes. We heard that 12th Street was packed with looters and the riots of '67 were in full force.

Mama grabbed me and told Deborah to go find Mike. Just as she said that, my brother rounded the corner, and was coming down our block, dodging other folks who were pushing past him. Mike had an entire rack with bags of Better Made potato chips in his hand, grinning from ear to ear. "Look what I got," he beamed. Mama looked at him, as only a mother could, and told him, "Boy, wherever you got those from, you better take them back right now." Mike looked scared of the gathering crowds that had instantly turned into mobs, and even more scared of Mama. He took the chips back.

I began to see the few White people who lived on our block displaying a look that could only be described as terror. They went into their houses and locked themselves in. Later that night I began to understand their fear: some White folks were getting burned out of their houses by Black people throwing Molotov cocktails. I began to fear for them as well. What would happen, for example, to my White friend with the flowers in her yard?

I knew that things would never be the same. A new divide was forming in my little head: an awareness of the division of people.

Neighbors who once lived in harmony now looked at each other with a suspicious eye.

We went inside and turned on the black and white TV. What we saw was made extra frightening because we could also hear it outside. It was like being in one of the tornadoes we heard so much about, except that we did not have a shelter to hide in. Mama had a set routine for that type of event and we always came out of it okay. We were smack dab in the middle of the riot. Sirens from the police and fire engines were constant, mixed in with gunshots and folks screaming "Black Power" and other slogans. Daddy finally brought Jr. home and then he left. So the four of us kids huddled around Mama for comfort. She provided direction and safety through this first, crazy, scary night.

As we watched TV, we saw how out of control and chaotic the city had become. The sirens and gunshots continued through the next day. We saw out the windows the mobs of people running by carrying stuff. As the second night carried on, I grew more and more fearful. I then heard on TV that there had been a Black man who was shot down for no reason by a White policeman and this is what started the riot. I was too young to understand or know that this period of time was wracked with gunpowder just waiting to explode. In fact, it had already exploded in other cities across the country.

We heard that White folks in the neighborhood were getting out, fearing for their lives. The little old lady with the garden was gone, plucked out in the very beginning of the riots by her family. Some of the White folks were told to paint "Soul Brother" or "Soul Sister" on their door to show that they were good folks and should not be threatened. A curfew was imposed: no one out on the streets and all lights out from dusk until dawn. I was terrified.

I woke up that next day and, with my child's mind, had forgotten the night and day before. I was ready to go outside to play like I had done every other summer day. But as soon as I saw my mother standing guard in the doorway, I could tell that this was no ordinary summertime. This was a pivotal turning point in my life. We could smell the smoke from the still-burning fires. We spent the day listening to my mom and the neighbors talk about the damage. They gossiped about who got hurt, which White folks made it out, who stayed, and what stores were burned out. This was just beginning.

Later that day we stood in the middle of our street and looked toward 12th to see nothing but flames. They were burning 12th Street down! There was a rumor of the burned body of a Black man found in the basement of the cleaners on 12th that really scared me. I had gone to this place with my mother. I had visions of our last trip there and the old guy who waited on us. I pictured him as he wrote out our ticket. I hoped it was not him that they found.

That evening we all gathered around Mama as she smoked her Pall Mall cigarette and looked out the front door. We had heard that the Army was being called in to help stop the riot, but we were not prepared for what we saw that evening. As we observed the curfew by not having the glow of the television on, we sat around anxiously waiting for whatever was next. It was eerily quiet and we could tell that the dynamics of the riot had changed. We could feel the shift in the air, like a bubble had burst and the gravity was slowly equalizing. It was still heavy with expectation. We sat on the couch trying not to be afraid. Suddenly, we heard the sound of very large, heavy-sounding trucks coming down the street, and a man shouted, "Put that goddamn light out!" My mom stubbed out her cigarette.

We all jumped up to get a peek at this scene. Coming straight down our street there was a line of National Guard tanks and jeeps. We were shocked, having never seen something like this before. The soldiers had big guns and rifles like in a war zone. I had no idea what it meant and it scared me something terrible. It shook my mom up too. She closed the front door and went into the back of the house in the kitchen and as we asked questions that she could not answer, she lit up another Pall Mall.

This was such a dark period in Detroit's history. Many people were hurt or killed. We heard all types of stories during this time: how it got started, how the police were beating anyone who was Black, how the National Guard was brought in by the President to stop the police from instigating and fueling the riots. There were some notoriously racists cops back then who were known to do shady things. This riot seemed to last forever in my young mind. Then it was over. I believe it was a turning point in my mom's life as well as in mine. Of course, I was too young to see the real backlash from the riots, just like I didn't see the match smoldering before the riots blew up.

Before that time there was enough Detroit for everyone. Everyone knew the rules. Then the race riot solidified them. For all the talk about creating good race relations, we were still separated. I was growing up and soon my perspective would change.

I first remember being cognizant of the reality of racism when I was about eleven years old. Our new neighborhood was a mix of races, and we lived on a block with more whites than blacks. We were now near Hamtramck; a Polish American town complete with Fat Tuesdays celebrated with jelly and cream filled paczkis (pronounced pawch-skis), and awesome meat pastries. Every day at school we placed our hand over our heart and recited the Pledge of Allegiance. "I pledge allegiance to the flag of the United States of America..."—pretty much saying that we were all one nation under God.

One day we decided to go to the famous bakery in Hamtramck on the other side of the train tracks where we sometimes placed a penny on the rail to see if a train would smash it. My sister, brother, and I got permission from Mama to go and we headed over there with a few friends. There was a chain link fence that separated the train tracks from the Hamtramck side, but we had discovered a broken piece where we could squeeze through and avoid walking the extra few blocks.

Once inside we stood around looking at all the goodies in the display case. I was really focused on that so I was not attuned to any of the surrounding tensions. We waited until two older boys in front of us were helped; I barely noticed that they were White. I decided on a chocolate covered donut. But on our way out, I noticed the two White teenagers standing there.

They were much bigger then we were. I am not sure what the teenager said, but our friend, Mike, reached up and punched him in his face. I saw the guy hit the ground and then I saw blood. Deborah grabbed my hand and we all took off running. Deborah and I went one way and the boys scattered. We headed to the opening in the fence. Running faster that I ever had before, I thought *I'm going to get shot in the back or something worse.* We got to the fence and I climbed through the hole. But I heard Deborah scream this loud agonizing wail and turned to see that a piece of the chain link fence was driven through her leg. She was bleeding, in pain, and stuck there. I could not pull the fence out of her leg. Not sure of what to do, we sat there and cried. I kept assuring her that it would be okay. The rest of the guys would see that we were not keeping up and they would come back for us.

Sitting there by the train tracks, waiting to be discovered by anyone from the train police to the Ku Klux Klan was terrifying. I tried to reassure Deborah. Just when I thought we would be there until the next morning, the guys found us. One of them held Deborah's leg while the rest of us pulled the link out of her leg. She was able to stand with help and we made it back home. We were full of mixed emotions. The guys were full of bravado but my sister and I were still shaking and scared, looking back over our shoulders. I don't even remember if we got our bakery items. I do remember feeling bad—for the boys back at the bakery, and for us.

My views on race were shaped over those years. During the riots I only saw one side of racism. I saw blacks angry—angry enough to hurt whites. What I heard for years was that whites had always hurt blacks. White people had us in chains and sold us as slaves and that's the story that I grew up with. I was too young to understand. But I really did not believe it would happen to me. Those types of things are not real until you have your own experience. I often heard my mom repeat one of her favorite sayings: "The white man is the devil." I never understood her because I had not yet experienced the White man as a devil. Eventually, I would be able to apply this saying to some men, both black and white.

FIRES, HOUSE, MOVING

After the riots everyone in our neighborhood was trying to move out. We ended up moving from the burned out West side of Detroit to Marcus Street on the East side. We moved into our first house, a nice place in a quiet neighborhood sandwiched between Hamtramck and the Chrysler Motor Company, Huber foundry. We had a three-bedroom home with a full basement and a garage out in the back. The upstairs had a bedroom where my brothers slept and another room that was very large. Deborah and I slept in our room downstairs and my mom's bedroom was at the front of the house. The kitchen was large, and we thought that was good until cleaning the kitchen became one of the assigned chores. This was a great place and we now had a better life. We had explored the area, rode our bikes, and met new kids. Mama made new friends, too. We came to know everybody in this neighborhood. Next door to us was a middle-aged Polish woman. I loved going over to her house because she had so many knickknacks ("chotskies," my mom called them)—little crystal figurines of houses, cats, and dogs. They were always dust-free and sparkled in the sun, casting a rainbow of colors.

These were times that I thought nothing bad could ever happen. Then we had the fire. We were asleep in our bedroom when it started. I was awakened to flashing red lights and banging on the front door. My sister and I ran to Mama's room to wake her up, and then upstairs to wake up our brothers, Mike and Jr. Rounding the top of the stairway, we could feel the heat. Looking out the back window I saw flames coming out of the garage. The heat was so intense that I felt it through the window. Mama had opened the front door to the fireman who was telling us to get out because of the possibility of the house catching on fire. Mama threw on some clothes and we all started out the front door. But then Mama turned back toward the bedroom and started searching the room, the drawers, everywhere. She said, "I have to find my false teeth." Those infamous teeth were always missing. Mama would drink a bit too much and then hide her false teeth. When she couldn't find them, she'd offer a reward to the child who could. Being the good child, I knew all of the hiding places. It was my job to sit by Mama's bed with the mop bucket while she got sick from drinking. I would empty the bucket when she was through which gave me an inside line on where she might put the teeth. On the night of the fire, I was able to quickly locate them. The garage burned down and we never knew how it started. Though the fire was surreal for me, I was not afraid. We developed a number of family stories and jokes from this incident, including Mama's lost teeth and my brother's strange choice of clothes that he grabbed in his haste to leave the house that night.

As children, we always found the humor after the fear and the pain. Though each of us had a different version of the events of that night, I'm sure we'd all agree that these were the best times of our lives.

Thankfully, Mama believed that everyone should have life insurance and home insurance. The insurance money Mama collected allowed her to put a down payment on another house that was even nicer and bigger than the Marcus Street house. So we went further east and nearer to Gross Pointe, the neighborhood we would visit at Christmas time to see the holiday lights. I loved everything about this new house: the kitchen where I would watch mama cook, the alley with a basketball hoop on the garage, the basement that had a bar and was paneled with wood. I loved to sit at the bar and feel grown up. Everyone was happy to live here.

Within a few months, our former neighbors, the Rhodes, moved around the corner from us and we continued our friendship with them. Life was good. I found a library and would walk the eight blocks every weekend to go and get armloads of reading material. School was great. I was growing up. There were new people to meet and new lessons to learn.

CHURCH MEMORIES

W hile I had a rich and full family life, spending time with my mama and my sisters and brothers, I also had a strong sense of myself as an individual. I had my own friends and interests that I nurtured over time, and I spent a lot of time by myself during the first decade or so of my life.

Directly across from our house lived the Wilsons. Keith was the oldest and he had two sisters, Vivian and Elaine. Their mom was single and very religious. My mom made a deal with Ms. Wilson to take us to her church on Sundays. It was fun and we got into a good routine of church for a while. Church was a great experience. People dressed up in their best clothes. The women wore fine dresses and huge, stylish hats. I would be decked out in dresses that twirled when I spun around real fast, which I loved to do! The preacher was very flamboyant and loud, telling us all about God's Kingdom, the one with many mansions with rooms for all of his children. Then there was the other side. The God of Moses who would strike you down if you did not obey the Commandments. I was very afraid of this God and all of his power. I vowed to obey all of the laws of the church and being the good child fit right in with that. I would get about fifty cents from Mama, Ms. Wilson, or Mrs. Rhodes to put in the collection basket. We would be allowed to take a nickel to buy penny candy. We also stayed after the prayer service for the food: fried chicken, greens, mashed potatoes, and other delicious good cooking that was prepared and served by the ladies in white. These women in white scared me a little bit. They stood on the outskirts of the pews during the service, fanning themselves and passing out fans to the other women who, either because they were older or fatter, looked like they were going to pass out.

It was also their job to come to the rescue when someone would get the Holy Ghost. This event was frightening to watch. It could only happen when the preacher was giving his sermon or when the choir was singing. There would be so much frenzy in the church that the Holy Ghost would fly down and enter some unsuspecting parishioner like a bolt of lightning. This person would start slow and build to a hysterical state. This usually meant singing, crying, and eventually falling or being gently led down onto the floor in a seizure-like state while the women in white crowded around the person, fanning them with their cardboard-on-a-stick fans.

This went on for about ten minutes and church was expected to continue through someone "catching" the Holy Ghost. Well, I never wanted the Holy Ghost. In fact, I was deathly afraid of getting it and I think most kids felt the same way. It was kind of a rule that it could only happen to older members and there was, it seemed, a time limit. You could not keep the Holy Ghost too long 'cause I guess he was busy and had a lot of people to visit. When he came, it was a sure sign that God was present and he was in the church, which meant that the preacher was doing a good job.

Sometimes we went to choir practice with the Wilsons. Ms. Wilson was a great singer. This is where I learned my favorite hymn that has stuck with me my whole life. "I went to a meeting one night, and my heart wasn't right! Something got a hold of me. I knew it was the Holy Ghost! He's my rock, my sword, my shield. He's my wheel in the middle of a wheel. I know he can, and I know he will, fight my battles if I just keep still. I got to trust him, trust him, and trust him. He's all right! One thing I know, the man is alright." I could not know it then, but for forty years these words would be my help through deep times of need.

My mother never went to church with us. And eventually there was no "us." It was just me going to church with the neighbors. Being "the good child," I never complained like the other kids. I just got up early on Sunday, put on my nice clothes, and waited for the Wilsons or the Rhodes to pick me up.

At some point during all of this I was also enrolled in a catechism class at the large local church, St Cyril. My mom was "Catholic" whenever anyone asked, but she never practiced it. I could only think that it was because I was so special that I, instead of my siblings, got to go. This class met every Saturday morning in the large gym of the big church. There were about seven of us little girls with the nuns. I don't remember learning too much about the Catholic faith. But I do remember one time when we were all sitting on the cold, hard floor of the gym and the nuns were explaining how "God loves everyone the same." I got the feeling that they meant everyone in the gym except me.

We were spread out around a single, huge sheet of paper to draw a message of God's love. I sat down next to the paper and began drawing rainbows, clouds, and bright yellow suns with rays of light coming out. I felt very artistic. As I admired my work, I suddenly got a weird feeling. I looked around and all the other girls were sitting as far away from me as possible. I didn't get it at first. Then they noticed me looking at them and one of the girls said in an entitled, racist voice, "My mother says I can't sit next to no niggers!" The nuns did not say anything to correct her; this bothered me most of all. I expected them to say something like, "Now Susie, we are all the same children in God's eyes." Instead, they just looked at each other, whispered among themselves in confusion, and proceeded to ignore the elephant sitting in the middle of the gym floor.

I continued to color and took my silent revenge by noticing how much better my drawing looked compared to theirs. I continued to attend and complete catechism, but as a separate participant. I felt ashamed for them. I was a little girl who knew even then that God did love us all. Now he loved me a little more because I was his and mama's good child.

Everything I learned about God I learned from Mama and the preachers. Mama had her belief that God should be feared and obeyed; she believed in avoiding the basic moral sins like lying, stealing, and committing murder. I later learned from preachers that there were crib notes of what not to do titled, "The Twelve Commandments." Being the good child, I was sure I would be able to follow them all.

STICKS AND STONES

I was an awkward child, tall and very skinny. There was a very well known soul singer, Joe Tex, and he had a hit song called "Skinny Legs and All." My family somehow made that my theme song. There was a line in the song: "Who will take the woman with the skinny legs?" Of course no one would want me, or so I thought. I was this very dark-skinned child, too, so this combination of attributes made a great platform for teasing including being called "blackie," "giraffe," "skinny," "bucktooth" (because of my thumb sucking), and "baldy" (because of the bumping of my head on the couch back on Seward Street).

I knew at an early age how to retort with the phrase: "Sticks and stones would break my bones, but names could never hurt me." When the teasing would get me down, or if Mama heard one of my siblings teasing me, she would offer her catchall phrase and philosophy on life. This covered everything from race relations, civil rights, and sibling rivalry. Mama would look at us with those sweet but stern eyes and say, "You ain't no better than anybody and ain't nobody better than you!" At the time, I thought that most of the teasing rolled off. I didn't understand why I had so many tease-able characteristics, but I knew that there was nothing I could do about them. But I was to realize later that all of these taunts were just hibernating, developing, and creating low self esteem that would surface later in my life.

My hair had been damaged from the process of straightening it with a hot comb. Hot comb straightening was a common practice among black folks. This involved taking a metal comb and placing it on the eye of a stove, directly in the fire so that it would heat up. Taking this hot, smoking piece of metal and combing it through the hair would turn kinky, nappy hair into silky, straightened hair. The black woman who created this process would go on to become the first black female millionaire. There is a fine line to this process, though: too much heat caused breakage and damage. My mama tried to help by taking me to a professional hair salon for treatments, but it would be years before my hair recovered.

Once we moved to Marcus Street, elementary school was not really any different from Seward Street. I continued my love of books; I got over my nylon fetish; and I made new friends. Most days after school, I made the rounds on our block, visiting everybody to see what was going on at their houses. People were very welcoming back then.

The Rhodes family became an integral part of our little group of families. They had taken me to church, too, alternating with the Wilsons. Mr. and Mrs. Rhodes had three children: Sam, Beverly, and Randy. Sam had a crush on my sister Deborah, and I had a crush at different times on Keith and Randy. Back then most families were whole. I would go over to the Rhodes house and hang out. I would just sit on the porch, or I'd watch Mrs. Rhodes cook, which was very interesting because of the different things that they ate and because she made such delicious meals. The Rhodes were from somewhere "Down South," a place that I only knew of by general location and where everyone talked funny. Beverly Rhodes was older than I was and I liked to hang around her. Beverly and her mother had a way of teaching me things as they went about their day. They showed me how to cook fried chicken (southern style) and hot water cornbread. I even watched Mrs. Rhodes make chicken feet sandwiches for Mr. Rhodes. I couldn't wait to run home and tell that!

I now know that Mrs. Rhodes was a typical southern woman from Arkansas. She was plump with such a sweet smile, she laughed easily, and was always quick to mother or nurture me. I loved her like a mom and so did all of the kids on the block. Like all of the adults back in those days, they would love as well as discipline anybody's child all in the same day. Mr. Rhodes worked each day and only had time for his kids on the weekend. All the boys loved him because he organized a boys' baseball team through the Amvets post that he belonged to. The Amvets hall was near the church that the Rhodes attended. Sometimes I would go to church with Beverly and her parents, and then to the post after.

Mr. Rhodes would gather all of the boys in the neighborhood, including my brothers, and we would all go a few blocks away to Burroughs Junior High School where there was a large baseball field. This became the home team's practice field. This was great for me because I felt like an unofficial cheerleader and ball girl at the same time. Mr. Rhodes taught the boys how to bat, pitch, and run. He was a great coach. He gave them a place to be and he gave them discipline. For many of our friends he was also a father figure to those without a father in their life. I became jealous of that sometimes; I wanted someone to be a father figure to me also.

I learned how to swim at an after-school program. I took to the pool like a fish to water. I would be allowed to walk the four or five blocks to the pool during the week, and for half a day on Saturday. Most of the time it would be dark outside after I was finished. It was freeing having so much time alone. I realized that boys did not find me pretty and I knew that I would never be as attractive as my sister. That was okay. At that time in my life I did not really care about boys. They were only relevant as opponents: to be beaten on the basketball court, to be out-swum, out-raced, and out-climbed.

Climbing trees was another one of my passions. We lived in a neighborhood filled with all types of fruit trees. Apple, cherry, and pear trees made our neighborhood a fruit smorgasbord. The only problem was that most of the trees were in other folks' backyards. So sometimes a group of us would go on raids: sneaking into other yards to pick the fruit. It seemed like all of the cherry trees were in other people's yards. They were such sweet black and red cherries that we would eat until our fingers and mouths were blood red.

Inside, our house was always full. Not just with siblings, Mama, and—for a time—my Aunt Thelma, but there was also a heaviness.

I didn't feel free in the house; it was confining. I found it hard to be alone inside. We had an apple tree in our backyard and this was my sanctuary; I loved that big tree. Whenever I got upset, or wanted to be alone, I climbed as high as I could in this tree. I'd climb high enough to look over the rooftops of all of the houses in the neighborhood. I could see Huber Foundry behind my neighborhood and almost as far as the elementary school five blocks away.

Sometimes I would eat apples and pretend that I was in a faraway land where I was in charge and everybody had to listen to me. I would eat apples until my stomach ached. I had a favorite limb that was just wide and strong enough to hold me. I would lie on this limb and block out the world, like during the time I found out that the other kids in catechism did not like me because I was Black. Or during times when I felt rejected by the boys in my neighborhood because I was tall and skinny.

The apple tree was another place where I daydreamed about my future. I knew from church that God sees everything a person does. He sees it and he knows what is in a person's heart. This reinforced my desire to be the good girl. If I was good and did everything I was supposed to do, then Mama would love and give me attention, and God would love me and give me a good life. These were the rules. I never thought about being rich. I just wanted to have a nice family and a nice home when I became an adult.

Sometimes I sat in that apple tree for hours. There were times, lying flat on my back on a big branch, looking at the sky through the leaves, when I fell asleep. I believed that this tree was placed in my yard especially for me. There were times, too, when my brothers and sister would be sent to look for me. They would look all over the neighborhood and there I would be: asleep in the apple tree.

This was a time in my life when all of my memories collected and were crystalized. I remember every day spent in that neighborhood. I remember each walk with my mom to the beer store and each dime concert that we would put on in our garage to raise money for candy. My sister and brothers and I were going to be the next Jackson Five.

My mama met a nice couple from Canada and in her continued effort to expand my window on the world, she allowed me to have sleepovers at their house. I thought of it as an international student exchange program. I would pack a bag and they would pick me up in a car very early in the morning. It always felt like a dream, being spirited away in the predawn hours to drive to Canada. We would drive to downtown Detroit and enter Canada through the Detroit- Windsor tunnel. I did not have a passport to enter Canada so they would use my Social Security card to gain entry. It was always tense going through customs: a White Canadian couple in the front seat with a Black kid in the back.

Once there, the sun would just be rising and I marveled at the different stores they had. We would drive for an hour and pass farms with tall corn growing. I felt as if I was specially chosen to get to experience this. Once at their home, our cultural exchange began. I learned how to make and eat tomato sandwiches, and they learned that I straightened my hair with a hot comb. They also learned that once we went swimming in their round pool in the backyard, my hair would curl back up. I gave them nappy hair and good hair lessons.

They had a daughter who was just a bit younger than I was. She loved my hair and I loved hers. We took turn playing with each other's hair. At night, if my hair had been straightened, she would help me roll it back up in pink sponge curlers. It took about thirty of these small curlers to roll all of my hair. This is what I did to my hair when I wanted to feel pretty. These trips to Canada seemed normal and I didn't really have many thoughts about Whiteness and Blackness. I loved these people like a second family. I always looked forward to those weekends: it was my idea of a perfect family.

There was a period of time before we moved from Marcus Street when I went through a very bad experience with joint pain in my legs. Mama took me to the doctor but they couldn't figure out what was wrong. They did not know what to make of my pain. The doctors said that the symptoms might be growing pains. Mama would give me aspirin but it was no match for the leg and joint pain that I felt. This was unbearable. All I could do was lie in bed and cry. Jr., who was already in High School, took me upstairs to his room and gave me reefer to smoke. He said that it would make me forget about the pain. I remember puffing on it and just when I thought it was not working, I drifted off onto a cloud. I continued to smoke during the pain. I eased my agony by smoking marijuana and reading a Hans Christian Anderson fairy tales book that Jr. bought for me one Christmas. And this is what got me through what became known as a Sickle Cell Crisis.

There was a test for sickle cell anemia but no one knew much about it because it was a newly discovered disease. Later, Mama had us all tested, and Mike and I tested positive for the trait. This meant that when we got old enough to have our own kids, there was a one in four chance that they could have the disease if the other parent also had the trait. I had the sickle cell trait but back then it was believed that only those who had the actual disease could have the excruciating joint pain crises. Thankfully, my bout with this disease did not last long. But as with so much in my life, I would circle back to this experience to help me at another point in the future.

I had a few real friends that I hung around with and we sometimes met up after school to talk and study. Karen came from a large family who lived in a modest home. She was a good friend to me and we hung out a lot both at school and outside of school. We were both interested in swimming and so we both enrolled in lifeguard training. Elaine was the friend with whom I'd go to the library. Another girl, Vanessa, was less like me and really quite interested in my brother. She lived in a large brick home in a better neighborhood near the Detroit River. I thought

Vanessa was lonely because she was an only child. I would go to her house after school and we would sing and dance to music.

I was thrilled to be invited by Vanessa to the junior high picnic at Bob-Lo Island. On this particular trip, the kids brought alcoholic drinks like beer and Right Time, a wine cooler drink that was the latest cool thing. Some of the even more advanced kids had marijuana. I was only interested in the drink. I thought it would make me look cool. I had experienced being tipsy before. Cleaning up after Mama's gambling parties, I would often drink from the leftover glasses or would be allowed to slurp the foam off of the head of a poorly poured Black Label beer. I also had experience with the reefer, but being the Good Child, I was not willing to be a drug addict. On the trip, I only drank a little bit of the wine coolers. She would question me about my brother and we got along just fine.

I was a very good student. This was part of the Good Child thing that I had going on. I found out early what the secret to school and good grades was. If I was there everyday, paid attention, asked questions even though I knew the answer, and did the homework, it was almost impossible to get bad grades. I was the teachers' pet and the kid in the class that everybody hated because I would ask for more homework. I was always fully engaged in my school studies and extracurricular activities. Once we moved from Marcus to our new house on Lenox I continued pursuing my certification as a junior lifeguard. I was like a fish in the water and I could dive like a pro. I also played in the forward position on the school basketball team where I was told I showed promise and that it might be possible to continue the sport into high school.

On some days I would come home for lunch instead of meeting friends. My mama would make me soup and a sandwich. I felt special like White kids must have felt. I'd seen those types of families on television. Those were the shows where they all sat down to dinner and passed the "Bu-tter." Those were the television shows where the mother was always wearing a white apron, and had a motherly answer for everything. When my mom made me lunch, that's how I felt. Like this would last forever: nothing but sunshine and good times.

MAMA'S GONE

ne particular evening, my cousin Linda came to pick me up for an overnight. This was nothing out of the ordinary. But I had no idea that this would be the last time that I would see my mama alive. I hugged Mama's neck and kissed her goodbye. She looked as good as always, smiling at me. "Be good, Brenda," were her last words to me. That wasn't a problem; I was always good for Mama. "Good" was not what I was. It was *who* I was. Good little Brenda: straight-A student, well-behaved, never back talking, never out of line, never the bad child.

Sometime the next day, Linda received a telephone call that my mother had suffered a heart attack. My cousin didn't tell me right away. There were more calls back and forth. Then she called her husband Mason at work and I could not believe my ears when she said, "Lil is dead." Then she broke down and started crying. The hole in my stomach was deep and black. I did not yet have what I could call "sadness." I simply could not comprehend this news. I could not process what was being said. But I did have a lot of dread. I withdrew within and somewhere I felt that this could not be possible. It could not be true. They had it all wrong. I kept thinking to myself, "Not my mama. They must be mixed up."

I had to get home, to show them that it was all a lie and it was not my mother. My mama could not die. She would never leave me. Then it hit me like a ton of bricks: the hole in her heart! She warned me about this over and over again. But I must have more time with her. Maybe by the time I get home she will be home from the hospital, all patched up. Maybe they could put a patch on it, like a bike tire, and give me back my mama. The forty-five minute ride from my cousin's in West Detroit to where my family lived in East Detroit felt like it was taking days. Riding in the back seat looking out of the car window, I just could not imagine how the world could continue to go on. Trees continued to blow in the wind, people laughed, children played. How could this be possible? Didn't the world know that the worst thing possible was happening? How could other lives continue? I had to get home to prove that this was some sort of bad dream. Or even worse, a cruel joke.

Mama would be there when I got home for sure, like she always was. If I closed my eyes, maybe it would all pass by the time I opened them again. Then came my flood of prayers: *I'll be better than good, God. I'll do anything. What do you want? Just let my mama be there when I get home. Please, please, please, God!* The car ride was deathly silent. We passed by the familiar places along our route. The sun was shining and I felt as if I would suddenly wake up and it would all be over. I had no tears. Why cry when this was either a dream or some fool's idea of a joke. No tears were needed. My mama loved me special. She would not leave me. Not yet. I was still just a child. Everywhere I looked I saw her smiling at me and telling me to be good. *I'm being good, Mama. Now you hold up your end of the deal.*

When we got to my house, there were many people there. I knew some but not all of them. I knew when I saw my daddy that this was real. My mama was gone. Still, some part of my brain just could not accept this. It was like a dream. I was in shock and did not know it. Some of the people I knew hugged me and told me that it would be alright; they gave me that grief look. It was the look that said, "Brenda, your mama is gone and your life will never be the same again."

Funeral plans were being discussed. I went upstairs to join Deborah, Mike, and Jr., who were all crying. I finally asked the one question that nobody seemed to be addressing. In a tiny voice I asked: "Who's gonna take care of us now?" My oldest brother said in a very earnest, grown up voice, "I will. Mama made me promise before she died that I would take care of her baby." Though he would try to live up to this promise, that fact that he was not able to follow through with it was just a lie that he would tell himself. Walking back downstairs was like walking through a dream. People were standing around talking.

This was the way death was handled in a black home. Neighbors and family gathered to remember the deceased. It all started off very solemn. A few hours later someone would open a bottle of liquor and the solemnness and grief would be replaced with laughter and memories being recalled about life with the deceased. I didn't understand. My mama was gone. How could they laugh and drink and party. I looked at the people who dared to be happy. It should have been impossible given that my world had crashed and life as I knew it was over. I could not believe my eyes or ears. It was a party: music, drinking, smoking, and laughing. How in the hell could that be? There in the middle of it all was my father, holding court, entertaining his subjects, and standing in tall cotton. Somebody saw me standing there watching and I was ushered back upstairs.

No one was answering any of my questions. I wanted to know what happened to my mama. And, what would happen to us now that she was gone. I wanted the familiar structure. I wanted reassurances. I wanted her to come back. For some time, I withdrew into my own little world. I believed that she would come back. She would not miss my walk into my teens. She would not leave me because she knew how important that was. *Who would answer these questions? Who would guide me from here on out?*

The funeral was like a slap in the face. I could no longer live in my fantasy world. Seeing what my mother looked like in a casket finalized her death. I did not want to go to the funeral. I had never seen a dead body before. I sat there in my seat during the family-only viewing of the body. There were flowers everywhere. Anyone who knew my mother knew that she hated flowers. Where was God? Why had this happened? She looked bigger than she was. Her face was swollen with death. During the service, I don't remember anything the preacher or anyone else said. I remember my mother's brother being there and I distinctly remember not liking him at first sight. I got the feeling that my mom was the black sheep of the family, unmarried with four children. *Now she's dead and they have a drunk for a father.* I knew that he would not be the one taking care of us. There was a moment to walk past the casket to pay last respects. Linda went over and kissed my mother on the cheek. Then she broke down screaming and crying. I remember I just wanted to melt inside myself, to just be zapped away to another place and time. This could not be happening to us.

Someone told me that when we walk through the line to view the body, we should kiss Mama on the cheek. The purpose of this was to keep her ghost from haunting us. That's some scary shit to tell a little girl about the mother she loves! Why would she haunt me? She loved me special. I was too afraid to kiss her but more afraid of what would happen if I did not kiss her. It was soon time. Time to get up, to follow my brothers and sister. I walked up to the casket with lead feet. They dressed her in something old-fashioned. I didn't think that she would have picked it herself. They had put make-up on Mama, but my mama never wore make-up. Every blue moon she might have had a touch of lipstick. They got everything wrong. I was so close to her. I desperately wanted to shake her and say, "Mama, come on! Mama, get up! Get up so that you can take care of me!" *Lord, why my mama?*

Mama did not get up and come home with us. We got back to the house and, again, there were a lot of people. It's strange how folks act after a funeral. Black folks like to look at death as a celebration. A "going home party," it's called. Going home to Jesus. In my Father's house there are many mansions. All I could think about was that Jesus did not need my mama more than I did. How could these people be drinking and celebrating my mama leaving? How could my daddy bring Ms. Mary here to my mama's house? Everyone was having a good old time drinking and celebrating. *This was no celebration for me.*

During the festivities, I got a call from Randy Rhodes. He tried to comfort me. I remember having the phone in my hand. It was one of the old-fashioned, heavy, black phones with the handle that had a stretched out cord. Stretched out by us kids "rapping" on the phone. My dad walked into the room. "You been on that phone a long time, Girl" he said. I looked at him, muttering under my breath so that he could not hear me, "You ain't my mama! You don't tell me what to do!" This was the first order from my father that I disobeyed.

I found out later that the paramedics had revived Mama twice, but then she suffered a stroke on the way to the hospital and they could not revive her a third time. *My mama loved me special. She would not leave me.* I was overwhelmed with sorrow. Everybody got to be a teenager except me. And in my mind, it didn't happen because my mother died before I turned thirteen years old. Surely, she would wait to see me become a teenager. There was still so much for me to learn and so much I wanted to know. I had so much to ask Mama, so many questions about my body, my sex, and—most importantly—my feelings. Where would I get those answers? Who would tell me? Mama was the only person who cared enough about me to take that kind of time to teach me. Because I was suddenly and unexpectedly shoved into a life without parental guidance, and because my mother was not there to help me move into female adolescence, typical life as a teenager simply did not exist for me.

GOOD GIRL GONE BAD

—⊰⊱⊰⊱—

This is where my story turns. It was the beginning of an End. We bounced around living from house to house; this had left me scared. I felt that at any moment someone was going to break through the door and get me. I had not known violence like that and a deep fear was all around me. I always felt unsettled. My father was around for a while, but then Daddy left and life got in the way.

We moved from the house on Lennox where we'd been living with Mama. During this time right after my mom's death, I felt like we were hobos. Daddy was drinking quite a lot, so we moved from place to place. We still had our large German shepherd named Buzzard. We ended up in a house that really was just a shell. It seemed, from the outside, to be vacant and partially boarded up. It was off of Mack Avenue, one of the worst areas in the city. There was no running water. We had no furniture and we slept on a dirty mattress on the floor. It looked abandoned and vacant from the outside. This shack had debris and tall weeds in the front and back yards. Because there was no toilet we went to the bathroom outside in the weeds. But this was really scary because the grass was full of critters scurrying about. Wood and glass were strewn throughout the inside of the house, along with an old couch. We were sure that there were rats. There were times when I tried to continue going to school. I would come back to this place after school and if other kids were around I would walk past the house so that nobody would know that I lived there.

My sister Deborah was having sleeping problems. We did not know it at the time, but she was having seizures. We only knew that she could not wake herself up. So my job was to watch her, and as soon as she started seizing I would wake her up. We both thought that she would die in her sleep. Her breathing was labored, and I would lie there hoping and praying that she would not die too. During these times, I would also watch the fleas jump back and forth between Buzzard and me.

There were many arguments between my father and my oldest brother George. My dad did not live with us in this vacant house. He had people that wanted him. He dropped us off and would disappear. He would either go back to Ms. Mary's house, or hang out with his drinking buddies. Ms. Mary would let us stay one or two nights at her place, but she always made it clear that she could not take care of us four children. I got the feeling that she tried to encourage my father to straighten up so that he could take care of us. I wondered, does an alcoholic have the ability to just straighten up?

Nobody else wanted us. Much later I learned that there was a possibility that I could have been placed in a foster care home because of my age.

I'm not sure how long we drifted between that ratty, vacant house and Ms. Mary's. My brother got a job at the Chrysler foundry and began to help take care of us. We ended up moving to a nice house on Manistique Street. All of us were living there, except for Junior who had enlisted into the Air Force.

I thought things would work out here. I started junior high school in the fog of grief, but I remember school being tolerable. There were a few good times at home, too, like listening to Al Green songs and the time my dad cooked Thanksgiving turkey while we were out only to return to see that Buzzard had eaten it. That winter we went shopping for coats and I picked out a long, midnight blue one trimmed in white Santa Claus fur. I loved that coat and I felt so unique when I wore it.

One day in junior high, I was called into the counselor's office and told that I had an opportunity to go Cass Technology High School, one of the most prestigious schools in the state. Cass only accepted the best and the brightest. I was so excited; I knew I was very smart and this opportunity proved it. I got back to my classroom and told my friends and my math teacher. I never went. Decades later, I lay in a hospital bed delivering my first baby and I remembered that opportunity. I thought about how my mama should have been there to guide me, how somebody should have cared enough to pay more attention to me and to what was going on. Deep down I knew that Cass Tech was an opportunity lost forever and that this baby would change the course of my life.

There were times when I would dream and everything was alright. Mama was there at the kitchen table making me a lunch of half a ham sandwich and half an apple. I could taste the cheese and Miracle Whip that was spread on the sandwich, the fresh white Wonder Bread that promised to help build my body 12 different ways. I could see the strawberry Kool-Aid and a tall ice-filled glass. Just then I would go to her longing to hug her and ask her where had she gone, why had she left me. She would get farther and farther away.

In waking life, I began to withdraw. On the outside I believe I looked okay. But I felt like I had been kicked in the stomach and the foot was still there.

For a short time, I thought I was starting to get back to normal. I was going to school, trying to pay attention, not worrying about whether or not Daddy was coming home. I was just trying to continue to be a good girl. But at some point, Daddy left and never came back. I should've seen this coming because there were times when he would leave and be gone for days, then he would call me and direct me to the three hundred and fifty dollar set of encyclopedias that Mama had bought before she died. This set of books contained all kinds of information and must've taken months for Mama to buy on the installment plan. When we first got them I would pick a letter, sit on our couch, and learn about everything from Pennsylvania to ponchos. Daddy would hide bail money in these books. He knew he would end up in jail, usually for driving while drunk. He would use his one phone call to tell me what letter to look in. I would get the money, catch the bus to downtown Detroit's courthouse, and bail him out. I remember doing this for the first time when I was thirteen and I felt like I was doing something grown up, and that only I could do for my daddy. I liked being the good girl. When Daddy was released, he'd take the bus back to Ms. Mary's and I'd ride home alone, not realizing the slight. This off and on disappearing continued for a while, but I guess the alcohol and the logistics got the better of him and he finally just quit coming home at all.

My second to youngest brother Mike and I were the only kids left at the house now with Jr. in the Air Force and Deborah in her own apartment after one too many name-calling arguments with Daddy. Deborah's escape plan had always been intact: she had worked for an insurance company straight out of high school. I felt so alone. Mike often told me not to worry, that he would take care of me. But how could I trust that? I seemed to be the little girl with a broken family who everybody left behind. When the beautiful, caramel-skinned sister I adored moved into her nice, one-bedroom place, I figured I'd get to move in. When this didn't happen, I felt abandoned all over again and I didn't understand why I couldn't live with Deborah. Apparently, when Mama died it became every kid for herself.

After Daddy left it felt like we had some freedom for a while. Day and night my brother's older friends would come over with beer, wine, weed, and music. I could try to drown out the pain. I drank and smoked until I passed out. But I could not erase the memory of my mother. Once Mike realized that Daddy really had abandoned us, he went into action. He thought that he could take care of us with the help of the welfare system and his minimum wage job as a security guard at a clothing store in Detroit.

Back then, the State of Michigan welfare application and evaluation process was a very long and tedious process. Reform to the system didn't come for years; when it finally did, the process would be seen as discriminatory. But Mike and I would walk to the Social Services office several blocks away and sit there for hours, for several days in a row. The childhood angst I'd feel when the social worker came to inspect our Seward house returned. I felt like we had done something wrong to deserve being poor. I sat there feeling so helpless. Finally, we were given two food coupons. We learned the system from the regulars: what benefits to ask for, how to answer the questions, how to behave with the social workers.

We were told that a determination would be made and we would get a letter. After waiting for what felt like forever, we received a letter asking for detailed information, utility and rent receipts, school records, check stubs. The process went on for months.

Meanwhile, we did not have anywhere to live so we stayed with friends. We were passed around from house to house.

I still wanted to be a good girl. But I was so mixed up. I didn't know how to act, how to be, or what was expected of me. I hung out a lot, just wandering around. Drifting. Trying to find my way. I didn't have any close friends to talk to. And I began to regret that Mama didn't show me stuff about being a woman. I discovered that no one stepped up to fill that role. For example, when my "journey into womanhood" began, I expected that my sister Deborah would teach me how to deal with this. Instead, I was given the tools with very little instruction. I was left to try to figure out this phase of my life and body just like I would have to in the future. This and other events regarding my body would leave me feeling ashamed and frustrated.

One of the places I lived after Daddy left and before Mike and I got on welfare was with the Rhodes family, our longtime friends with whom I'd spent so much time going to church and learning about southern cooking. The Rhodes were good country folks. They had simple values and rules. They did their best to give me a stable place to live. They shared my sadness, and had pity for me. They really cared a lot about me and understood the gravity of losing Mama more than I did. Beverly Ann, the daughter whose room I shared, tried to make me feel welcome.

After Mama died it seemed that I couldn't give myself away no matter how hard I tried. I was just so lost. I went downhill very fast like a rocket falling to earth. I began to take on the world in my own way. I began to act out.

I would smoke weed with a guy who lived across from the Rhodes. Sometimes we would make out but he would never let it go too far. I was fifteen years old and really wanted to have sex; I think I really just wanted to feel loved and special. The more rejected I felt, the braver I got to try things that I never would have considered before my mama died. Beverly knew people who would give her pills; she sometimes shared them with me. I popped every pill from black beauties, to Valium, to whatever I could get my hands on. But the thing that ultimately got me kicked out of the Rhodes' home was what I did with Beverly's brother, Randy. Mrs. Rhodes had told me that I was to leave her son Randy alone, knowing that he and I had been sweethearts off and on when we were younger. Though Randy had long since told me that I wasn't his type, living in the same house gave us an opportunity to sneak around at night. We'd go to the basement to make out and mess around. When Mrs. Rhodes caught us, that was it for me. I was so ashamed of myself for hurting the one person who was still willing to treat me kindly. I did not know how to tell Mrs. Rhodes how sorry I was, so I just stayed away and continued my downward spiral.

I stayed with another family briefly, followed by staying with Linda, my brother Jr.'s girlfriend, at her mother's, on the west side of Detroit. That neighborhood of high-class black people who didn't like poor black people like me, was really foreign and I felt like a fish out of water. Mike and I were allowed to live in their nice, finished basement. We moved in the few things we had packed into boxes and a few clothes. They had rules we were to follow: no entering the upstairs, no opening the refrigerator, no eating after Linda's mom came home. She did not want to see or hear us while we were there. She was a hard worker who was always in church on Sunday. Appearances were important. But I would go upstairs anyway and listen to music with Linda. She would talk about my brother and the wedding she hoped to have with him. And she would talk about my mom. Sometimes we would go down to a nearby park to convince somebody to buy liquor for us. The last week that Mike and I lived at Linda and her mom's house, it rained so hard that water flooded the entire neighborhood, including the basement. All of our belongings were destroyed and we couldn't stay there anymore.

But no matter which pills I popped, how much weed I smoked, or what I chose to drink, it never changed the fact that my mama was gone. It never altered how I was being shunted from home to home, that none of this was fair, or right, or even understandable. I had been abandoned, over and over again. I could not believe this was now my life. I could not get over the feeling that everywhere I turned my mother would just be coming around the corner. I really felt that if I just looked and prayed hard enough, if I just figured out what that one thing was that God wanted me to do, somehow my mother would come back. I couldn't believe that she would leave me.

Even after years had passed, I was not "over it." I couldn't believe that one day we were sitting in the kitchen while she made me lunch and the next day she was gone.

FALL FROM GRACE

D uring my childhood, my Aunt Thelma had come to stay at our house for a month. She had some disabilities that I could not name and I was at first afraid of her. But during that long visit, I learned that she had a great sense of humor and I began to smile at her a lot. Later I found out that she was mentally ill, had suffered a stroke, and lived with chronic asthma. Her daughter, my cousin Linda, had been married off to a man thirty years her senior when she was still a teenager. Linda and her husband Mason lived with their children on the far side of Detroit. That's where I had been on the day they told me my mama had passed away. After my mom died, Linda never offered to let me live with her. But I did continue to visit sometimes.

Linda never got the chance to finish high school and could not read very well. When she got any important looking mail she would phone Deborah or me to spell out the words for us; we would write it all down and read it back to her. Most were offers for sweepstakes and other nonsense. Sometimes she saved them up and on the weekends we would go over and spend time reading her letters. She eventually learned how to read enough to get by. She learned how to read as her children learned.

I remember the weekend they came to pick me up to take me back to their house. Linda was just like a big kid and all about fun. We would drive around during the daytime flirting with young guys. At night, we would play games or call strangers from the phone book and flirt with them. This particular weekend, I had called Linda crying because my steady boyfriend Johnny had just broken up with me over

55

the phone because I wouldn't have sex with him. Though I begged him not to dump me and promised to do what he wanted, he and a girl he said *would* have sex with him laughed at me and hung up. I felt ashamed of still being a virgin. I was humiliated. And, once again, I had the feeling that no one wanted me. Sixteen and never been touched. The good girl. This good girl shit didn't seem to be working out for me in this life. I tried to be a good girl and to do everything that I was supposed to do. Wait to have sex until after you are married is what I was taught in sex education. This was just not working out. Linda told me that I should show Johnny that I was not just a good girl but that I was mature enough to have sex. Sex was nothing. I could do that. I never fully understood emotionally or physically what that meant or the toll it would take on me. I took a lot of my cues from my cousin. I told Linda my story about Johnny and she made it her mission to get me laid.

So we went out driving around neighborhoods. Linda stopped at a liquor store to buy me beer. I drank and she drove. We spotted this guy sitting on his porch. He looked like he was a few years older than me. We went around the block and drove by a second time to get a better look. Linda was notorious for shouting out of the car window using her sexy voice. "Hey, baby. Can we talk to you?" He came over to the car and Linda asked what his name was. She introduced me and told him that I was shy but that I was looking for some fun. I was sitting there sweating bullets. Linda told me to get out of the car to talk to him and then drove off "to give us privacy."

This total stranger and I sat on his porch for a few minutes. He asked me how old I was and I lied, telling him that I was eighteen. He laughed like he knew that was not true. We never got past the surface questions. Linda was back and I practically ran to get in the car. We made a date for Linda to drop me off the next day and then we went back to her place. That night Linda told me that I should lose my virginity to this guy, just get it out of the way, and that older guys know what to do unlike young boys like Johnny. I was afraid but I was glad that it seemed like this guy wanted me. The next day was sunny and hot so I had on shorts and a T-shirt. We went back to this guy's house and I knocked on the door.

Walking up to the door of this stranger's house I knew something was terribly wrong. It seemed like a big house from the outside but felt cramped and dark inside. Once my eyes adjusted to the dimness, I saw old furniture and a woman in her forties sitting at a table. The stranger-man quickly told me that was his mother. She sat there looking at me and it seemed like she had been put through hell, like she had worried for most of her life. She didn't speak to me.

She just looked like she felt sorry for me as if she knew what was happening to me. She didn't try to stop it. He took my hand and led me into his small bedroom. I tried to relax. But I was very, very nervous. He started kissing me. Before I could really get my bearings, things just sped up really fast and the next thing I knew my shorts were off. He was like a madman, panting hard like a wild dog. Then there was a very sharp pain and I screamed really loud. I said, "Stop!" I said, "No, I don't want to do this." I tried to prevent it from happening because I was terrified. I was sure his mom would hear me screaming. He put his hand over my mouth and he just kept on going until he was done. After it was over, I lay there crying for a few minutes.

When we got back to the house even Mason knew something bad had happened. I stumbled into the house and went upstairs. I soaked in a bath and cried. I felt very dirty. My good girl status had gone right out the window. That was the end. That rape took all of the goodness out of me, it seemed. I just kept wondering what Mama would think. From then on, every action I have ever taken always has that hanging over my head: what my mama would think. I felt like people could see my shame. This really killed the little girl that was trying to hold on. She was gone and never really had a choice in the matter. She never had a chance. And now, who could I trust? How could I trust myself? After that, sex really didn't mean anything to me. It took a while before I did it again and by then it was like my body was dead. Sex was a way for me to give myself to other people. It was the only thing I had that other people wanted. It was the only gauge for whether or not I was desirable. I never felt attractive. But I never knew that each time I had sex it would tear another little piece of me away. I was taking my cues from Linda because I didn't have anybody else to teach me. Weekends at her house meant doing the same things over and over, finding guys to flirt with. When she flirted with guys, I was her excuse to go out to be with them.

Around this same time, a moving company was started in the Detroit area, run by a family business. Cousin Linda knew one of the brothers in this family and she'd take me over to their house and then disappear into the next room with the man she was seeing. I was left in the main living area with another brother. On one such occasion, I began to open drawers in a bureau and saw all these ladies' undergarments. I was shocked and confused. What I found out much later is that the brother I talked with in the living room would be convicted as a serial rapist in the mid-1970s. He was arrested for raping and killing prostitutes that he would pick up along Cass Corridor. I can't imagine how lucky I was not to have been raped by this man. When his name appeared in the paper so many years later, I could not tell anybody that I had been in the same room with this guy and that I had seen the panties of women that he had raped and murdered.

Clearly, Linda was far from being a positive role model and I knew that I would get into real trouble if I kept hanging out with her. Eventually I started making excuses that I could not go over to see her. Then they weren't really excuses. She went through various illnesses but there was nothing I could do; I was spiraling down myself. I would see Linda occasionally through the years. We tried to stay in touch but things were never the same with us. I realized that she put me in so much danger all in the name of fun. I quit laughing when I realized I might have gotten killed.

I can still remember like it was yesterday the rape and losing my virginity, and I have been deeply scarred.

CHAIN OF FOOLS

S oon after the flood at Jr.'s girlfriend Linda's house, we were finally able to get the welfare help we needed: rent vouchers, food stamps, and cash. Mike found an apartment for the two of us at the Appletree Apartments on Jefferson Avenue. It was a very nice, new, one- bedroom place on the sixth floor. I slept in the bedroom and Mike slept out on the couch. We celebrated having a place to stay dry and clothes to wear. Mike was working and we were on welfare. The apartments had a nice lobby with marble floors and a row of locked mailboxes. We had a security intercom in the lobby so residents could decide whether or not to let somebody inside the locked complex. Attached to the apartment building was a liquor store. It seemed like the long hell of living with other folks was finally over. We had our own place. I thought I was okay. Drinking was our pastime, and we had a lot of friends to hang out with us. Mike had his usual steady stream of girlfriends.

I became hot and heavy with Thomas, the guy I had met through the neighbor, Barbara. At first, I thought that Thomas and I were exclusive. He never hid the fact that we were a couple. I felt so lucky to have such a fine boyfriend. He was tall and slender with brown skin, and he was definitely a smooth talker. What I didn't yet know was that Thomas was still sleeping with Barbara, the women I babysat for up until she found out Thomas had made a pass at me. Thomas told me that he needed to keep seeing her because she gave him money for drugs. Thomas would sleep with anyone for drugs or money, though he told me that he had stopped sleeping around.

I would spend the night with him and he would hold me, telling me stories about how our life together was going to be. We would get married, he would say, and live in a very good neighborhood. We would have two children, a boy and a girl. He would work so I would not have to and we would live happily ever after. He would talk me to sleep most nights and I felt safe in his arms. I blocked out the filthy house, welfare, drugs, mama being gone. Everything was okay when I was in Thomas' arms and I really wanted to believe we could have the life he described.

Then one day I got a really bad infection. There was nobody in my family I could ask about it. So I asked Thomas' mother what it could be and she told me that it sounded like gonorrhea. I was so mad, screaming, and very dramatic. Thomas was as calm as a cucumber. He told me that I needed to grow up, that these things happen. And how did I know I got it from him anyway? I could have given it to him instead. Well, that was not possible I told him. Then his mother went into her bedroom, came back out, and gave me a big bottle of penicillin. I took the pills. I was ashamed and humiliated, but grateful that I didn't have to tell my family. This was the first of many times that I found out about Thomas' other women.

I never really knew what Thomas did all day. I did know he shot dope because there would be times when he would return high. He would sit on the couch and nod off. I was so naïve that when he told me he was not addicted, I believed him.

I was embarrassed when Thomas would visit me at our apartment. Daddy was there one time when Thomas arrived just after shooting up. It was hard to ignore the fact that my boyfriend, and later the father of my child, was a dope fiend when he was nodding off and oblivious to everyone around him. Thomas would sit there with his head slowly bending down toward his lap. Then he would jerk back up, like nothing had happened. My father would later bring this up in an argument. His favorite description of Thomas would be used in a sentence such as: "Well, if you need diapers, tell that nigger you live with to stop slobbering on his dick and go out and get a job and buy you some." Yes, that's the way my daddy talked.

There was a doctor's office across the street from the Appletree Apartments where I lived with my brother, Michael, before all of the chaos of living with Thomas' family. Back then I went to any doctor who took Medicaid. It didn't matter if he was a good doctor or not, I needed a pregnancy test. When I found out that I was going to have a baby, I panicked. This proved to me that I was the bad child. *What would my mama have thought? What happened to her sweet baby girl? What would my life look like now?* The Good Girl lived in a house full of roaches in the ghetto and was pregnant with a baby whose father was a dope fiend.

I moved between excitement, fear, shame, and worry. As a pregnant seventeen-year-old, I imagined it could be fun to dress up a baby who would love me and be with me forever. But I cried when I got back to the apartment and told Mike. It had been such a long, hard road for the two of us. We had been abandoned and made to feel like a number by the social services department and I was adding a baby to the situation. But I felt special and alive for the first time in a long time, too. Here was something I could do. Mike ended up being my biggest supporter. He did not indicate that he knew much about the fights I had with Thomas. Of course, I figured that once I was pregnant the abuse would stop altogether. Mike made sure that I had everything I needed: bottles, a bassinet, blankets. He was happy about being an uncle. Deb too, while also not fond of Thomas, wanted me to be well and was excited about being an auntie. Daddy, on the other hand, was not happy. He saw that I was on a downward spiral as I continued on with the relationship with Thomas. I continued high school until I was eight months pregnant. At that point, I was too lazy to catch the bus. I had fallen in the snow once on the way to school, so I used that as an excuse. And just like that, I became a statistic in one fell swoop: pregnant and a high school dropout.

It was an uneventful pregnancy. I didn't have much morning sickness and my brother Mike made sure I didn't drink a lot. It was okay for my baby as long as I didn't drink liquor and smoke weed, so I drank beer and I smoked cigarettes, not knowing that there were consequences. Being pregnant gave me a good safe feeling like I was somehow protected and that I was protecting my baby. Thomas did not fight too much while I was pregnant and he never hit me. I thought I could stay pregnant forever. I loved this baby and really wanted her to stay in my womb; I felt so close to her that way. There were no signs of anything wrong. I got regular check-ups and ultrasounds and I kept a photo of the ultrasound with me because I was sure I could make out my baby in that fuzzy, black and white image. On March 3, 1977, Thomas had been driving us around the icy, snowy streets while he was high and we crashed into a fire hydrant.

Four hours later I went into labor and delivered a gorgeous baby, Tamiko Nicole Jones. I lay there in that hospital bed thinking about Mama and how sad I was that she would not see my child, her grandchild. I really wanted her there to comfort me. There was nobody to give me any idea of what to expect, or what to do now that I had a baby. I thought about all the choices I had made since my mama died. And I lay there blaming God, Mama, Thomas, everyone but myself. But I would show them all. I would give this little, tiny, baby girl all of my love. This child would have everything. I would be a good mother, and—most of all—I would never leave her. We were bonded in this life together and we would take care of each other until the day we died.

I brought Tamiko home to the apartment that Mike and I shared, and for some time it worked. It also seemed like Thomas was happy to have a baby. I began to drink a bit more after Tamiko was born. I also began to get depressed. My world got smaller; my bedroom in the apartment became my realm. After the newness of Tamiko wore off, I began to wonder what would become of us. Mike was working all day and Thomas was doing whatever he did over on his side of town. I recalled the way Thomas' sisters neglected their children and I made some promises right then. I vowed that my baby would not run around with snot all over her face, or with feet so black they look like socks.

I vowed to protect my baby from falling down the stairs or drinking poison. I promised that my baby would be clean and well-dressed all the time. I would be sure she knew she's loved. I vowed to never, ever leave her alone.

I should have stayed in the Appletree apartment with Mike and baby Tamiko, but I missed Thomas and eventually moved back to his mother's.

THOMAS, FAMILY LIFE

S oon I was living with Thomas at his mother's house. Dorothy, the matriarch, tried to be a good person, but she was not a good mother. Charles was the oldest brother and chief breadwinner; he worked at Chrysler Motor Company. Yvette, his sister, had a baby girl and liked to party. Often, we'd go out to bars together, drinking and dancing all night – even after I had my own baby. Yvette and I had a built-in babysitter, Dorothy. I always made sure my daughter was clean, fed, and safe before leaving her. There were also a few other sisters who lived there with their babies. We all just lived in that house together - in the filth of dishes piled high, floors that blacken bare feet, with roaches everywhere.

One day Thomas came home with a woman. She was a little bit older than me and very pretty. He introduced her to me and explained that she would be living with us. She would sleep in a separate room and he would distribute himself between us. We would be "sister wives." Of course, I did not like this. I argued with him, even threatened to leave. But Thomas took me aside and smooth-talked me. He told me he only wanted her for her money, so I agreed to her staying. It was difficult. I never knew if Thomas would be spending the night with me or with her. Thomas' sisters never let me forget how stupid I was being; they continually teased me about who would be getting Thomas on any given night. After a week of this, she blew up at Thomas and left. I thought I had won. I didn't see that I had won a liar and a cheat. I was so ashamed. But I was not ashamed enough to leave him.

I knew this was a shitty way to live but I chose to accept it. I was still glad that he wanted to keep me instead of her. At least he didn't get rid of me, right? He even put her in my bedtime story, talking about how she would come in handy for us and how we would use her for her money. There was an old saying, "find a fool, and bump his head," and that was exactly what he was doing. Thomas found her and she was willing to give him money. So he would continue doing that for as long as she let him.

The first time Daddy came over to Thomas' house to check on me I was totally unprepared. I saw him from a distance coming down the street. I had no idea that he knew where I was. I could tell it was my daddy because of the distinctive walk that he had. He "swaggered" before it was even a word. Tall and lean, one of his steps was like two of mine. He was always dressed neatly even when he was drunk. My dad had this mustache that prickled me when he kissed me on the cheek and collected food when he ate. At the time, I thought he had come to talk me out of spending time there with Thomas.

As my dad approached, everyone seemed to scatter to different rooms. I was not sure what to do. When he got to the porch, we went inside and I introduced him to Thomas. I was so embarrassed by the way the house looked: sparse furniture, beer cans strewn all around, and roaches all over the floor and walls. "How you making out?" Throughout my life whenever we spoke, this was exactly how Daddy asked about me. Though my dad never said anything about the way the house, the babies, or the kitchen looked, I could see in his eyes that this was not the life he had wanted me to have. Heroin addict boyfriend living with his welfare mom; my future did not look good. Daddy never stayed long, never offered to help, never said what I had longed to hear: "Come home with me and I will take care of you. You will be safe now, Brenda." No, I never heard those words. I always felt like crap when he came to see me over the years. I would be shaken up for a day or so vowing to get my life together, to leave Thomas, and to never return. That did not happen.

The first time Thomas hit me it was for something I said. I always had more mouth than necessary back then. But that was because my mouth was my only weapon. I was quick-witted and could use my mouth to cut someone down in an instant. Needless to say, Thomas did not like that. He slapped me so hard that I saw stars. I was completely shocked. I tried to fight back and it never dawned on me until it happened, that he was really trying to hurt me. At some point, I decided to stop fighting back to let him get it out of his system. I could see my mother on the floor, crouched in a fetal position as my dad kicked her. I thought to myself, "No, I will never let this happen to me again."

After he was finished, I lay there crying as he stormed out. Thomas' mother came in the room, passing him as he was leaving and said something stupid like, "Thomas, you know you should not be beatin' on that girl." Thomas was a smooth talker. After I quieted down and he had taken a hit of his drugs, he would return to tell me how sorry he was that he had hit me. He told me how I had just made him snap. It was always my fault. Of course I provoked him. I made him do it. Our fights started slow and grew. I always tried to fight back and then, afraid that he would break something or worse, I would assume the fetal position just like my mom. I left him over a hundred times in my mind but I never actually went anywhere.

I believe my brothers and sisters were affected by that night my father came into our house and beat my mother. Every fight with a boyfriend or husband would be a repeat of that night. Once I got hold of myself and stopped crying, I looked at myself in the mirror. Both of my eyes were red but the right one looked like a blood vessel had burst. My first thought was that I'd leave and this would never happen again. My second thought was about how I would explain this to Mike. I believed that if he knew Thomas had done this to me there was a possibility my brother would kill him. So, I learned how to lie about the abuse. But Mike had to have known that I could not be that clumsy.

So many doors I said I walked into; so many stairs I tripped up and down. Looking back at Mike's girlfriend Sharon, I realize she "tripped a lot" also and she often wore dark glasses. Sharon and I did not talk a lot about the similarities at the time, maybe because of the shame and guilt. The shame and guilt of staying.

I took Tamiko to the doctor for her six-month check-up. The doctor's office was small and there were not very many people waiting. Tamiko was being very good. We were ushered into a back room where the nurse weighed her and took her temperature. Blood was drawn which made her cry and then the doctor examined her. Tamiko looked very healthy. Though small for her age, she was gaining weight. The entire visit had been very uneventful. So I bundled her back up in her blanket, and off we went for home.

As I walked, I thought about what I was going to do with the rest of the day as I wasn't in school and had no job. I knew that I wouldn't do anything; I would just sit at home with Tamiko. When I got to the house, Dorothy told me that the clinic had called and wanted me to call them back. So I called right away. I could hear some panic in the nurse's voice as she told me that I needed to bring Tamiko back to the clinic immediately because of something about her blood tests.

I was worried but hoped that maybe they just needed another blood sample or something. So I bundled up Tamiko again and started to head out. Before I could get out of the door, though, I got a call back from the nurse instructing that I take my baby straight to Children's Hospital. She said Tamiko's blood count was extremely low and that she might need a blood transfusion. The doctor's office arranged to have a cab pick us up and drive us to Children's. I was watching Tamiko all the way to the hospital; she didn't look or act sick. I thought, maybe they got the results mixed up with someone else's. But I was very afraid. And it was then and there that I began to take responsibility for Tamiko's illness. Every runny nose, every scrape on her knee, each shot by a nurse, and every second of pain became my burden to bear.

I felt guilt, shame, and a general feeling of being unfit as a mother. Self-talk helped to cement this into my head. I had no business having a baby, none at all, it said. Now I was being punished for that. Tamiko would suffer for my sins, because I would not follow the rules, because I had not been the good girl. I kept these feelings inside but they were always close. I could feel them poking through my skin as if I were a piece of cellophane. I sometimes felt that others could see through me also. I always felt like doctors and family members were looking through my skin, judging me and finding me guilty of being unfit. I even felt my mama's judgment from her grave. Everyone looking at me and seeing that I did not know what I was doing. I was determined not to become what everyone thought I was and to take care of my baby until my last breath.

There was a period of Tamiko's infant life where she was very healthy, when she still had the protection of the baby hemoglobin, the super blood that God sees fit to give them to protect them from the world. Lord, how I often I wished that she could have super blood for her entire life.

The cab driver dropped us off at the emergency room entrance. I had no idea how this worked. I had never been in an emergency room in my life. I saw lots of miserable, sniffling, crying children, and exhausted looking parents. Little did I know that I was about to join the ranks, becoming one of the haggard regulars at the Children's E.R. As soon as we had registered, we were taken in to see the doctor; this is not a good sign in a place where the sickest children get seen first. That was my first indication that there was something terribly wrong with my baby. The first thing they wanted to do was to take more blood. Tamiko was screaming and I was doing anything I could to soothe her. They put her through a battery of tests and x-rays. Finally, they told me that Tamiko had sickle cell disease.

I flashed back to the day when my mother took us over to be tested for sickle cell. We loved to take the bus through the city. It was always a fun experience for us. We would run onto the bus, looking for empty seats, always trying to get the seat that was next to Mama. Being the baby, this was always my spot. By default, Mama would let me sit with her. I enjoyed the different people who rode the bus. There were people from all walks of life. There were folks going to and from work, people who were down on their luck, and folks with families and babies. I liked to try to figure out what was going on in their lives. It's amazing what a mind remembers when a person has been given incomprehensible news. At the time we were diagnosed with the sickle cell trait, I thought I would never have to worry about this disease. I don't know why I felt that way. Then I heard a voice in my head say, "You gave your baby girl sickle cell disease." That incessant voice went on and on. I still hear it nearly four decades later.

The doctor explained that Tamiko has a blood disease that was inherited because both of her parents have the sickle cell trait. Sickle cell disease causes pain crises. When blood cells lack oxygen they form the shape of a sickle and they get trapped in the blood vessels. I didn't understand the gravity of it yet. I didn't understand that it would mean hundreds of nights in crisis going to the E.R. for the rest of her life, up to the present day. I didn't understand all of the pain that she would be going through, all of the pain that I would be going through. In that moment the only thing I knew for sure was that I was going to take care of her. The doctors and nurses gave me information about the disease and we were admitted to the children's hematology clinic. I was instructed to only take Tamiko to the clinic at Children's Hospital so that they could follow-up with specialists to manage this disease. That was the beginning of a long, long road.

I didn't know anybody who had ever had the disease. I had never heard of anybody being sick with it, so I just continued on with our life. I wouldn't fear it because I didn't know what it was. I took her home and life continued until she had her first crisis, which was soon after she was diagnosed. It seemed to me like this disease was waiting to explode. As soon as they put a name on it, it started manifesting itself. That's what my little brain told me.

One night my baby just wouldn't stop crying and she was hot with fever. I tried all of the remedies I knew, but I did not have any go-to remedies for this new disease. I saw that her little feet were puffy red and swollen. She would not let me touch them. I knew I had to get to the hospital. Thomas never went to the hospital with me. During those first hospital stays, Deborah and Mike would come to visit. It was such a sad affair. Tamiko would be there and she would be in so much pain. Each trip was always like the first trip. Sickle cell is a critical illness because the pain crisis can cause heart attacks. Unless it was unusually crowded, Tamiko would be taken in right away. They wanted to get the pain under control. Anytime she had a fever, it entailed admission to the hospital with a minimum three days stay. This always included IV fluids to keep her hydrated. I would watch them put the IV in and just cry along with her. Sickle cell babies have a very hard time with their veins collapsing. Even then it was hard for them to find and keep a vein. Eventually, Tamiko got a permanent port put in her chest just so she could receive IV fluids and blood transfusions.

My baby. I could not begin to imagine this pain. She was so helpless. I didn't know how to feel. I tried to be strong for her. She had excruciating pain when she was only six and half months old. Nothing would help. It hurt so bad and there was nothing I could do. Tamiko and I were not prepared for any of this. The first time we were in the hospital I stayed there with my baby. She just needed me to hold her. There were too many times when I did have to leave her there. But I would always return and tell her that everything is okay. I'd hold her and we'd play and I would try to make her laugh. She didn't understand what was going on: why her feet hurt and why her hands hurt. She did not understand why she had to be put in a metal crib like a large dog crate. Most of all, she did not understand when I had to walk away. But sometimes I had to walk away so she didn't see me cry. I have to be strong because there is no one else. So I would go home and drink hard at all this pain.

Dorothy, Thomas's mother, had many men callers, which was strange because she was not a good looking or clean woman. The men would come to visit, drinking while Charles and Thomas scrutinized them the way sons do. Rick was the last of these men that I would meet. He was short, skinny, quiet, and needy. He would always try to steal kisses from Dorothy and she would giggle like a schoolgirl. But the courtship got old really fast and Dorothy told me that Rick was too clingy. When she broke it off with him one morning, he stormed off. Later that afternoon, though, Rick was back and I could tell that he had been drinking. Dorothy and Rick began to argue intensely to the point that he began to threaten her. Thomas and Charles stepped in to help get him out of the house, and as Rick was being pushed out of the door he threatened to come back to kill everybody in the house. Thomas retaliated with, "You better be packing heavy then." I was hoping that the threat was just crap. But everyone else in the house started preparing for safety; a few left for the night. Shortly after that, Thomas told me that he was going out to pick up a gun in case Rick came back.

At that point, it got real for me too. I felt trapped and angry. There was a heavy feeling of doom in the air. I hunkered down in the bedroom with my little baby, and Thomas returned with a sawed-off shotgun and a glassy-eyed high. I felt like I had a hole in the pit of my stomach. This was bad, really bad.

Just after finally dozing off, I was suddenly awakened by footsteps on the front porch. I grabbed my baby and lay huddled on the floor. Rick screamed for Dorothy and I heard him kick in the door. I peeked out through the open bedroom door and saw Rick standing with a gun. Thomas pumped his shotgun and fired at Rick. Then Rick's gun went off. I could smell the gunpowder and the iron smell of the blood. I screamed. The shotgun blast hit Rick midsection and he flew across the sidewalk, landing with his back up against a tree. I remember the look of happy shock that was on Thomas' face. He was hyped and laughing. It seemed as if I was stuck in a bad movie. Then it got eerily quiet. The police and ambulance came. Cops were questioning Thomas. They had him in handcuffs. Dorothy was crying hysterically. Chunks of body tissue were splattered on the porch and on the steps. Rick was dead.

How could I be involved with these people? These folks were killers. They knew Rick would be back. Thomas waited. He planned this. The police took all of us down to the station for questioning. The nightmare continued. How did I get involved with this? What would they do to me? What would happen to my baby? This would be a new low: going downtown to be questioned in a shooting case, with my baby in my arms. We were very quiet on the way down; we were all in shock. They questioned us one at a time about the shooting and I'm sure we all said the same thing. The police let everyone go except Thomas. He was charged with having a weapon while on parole (for shoplifting the year before, for which he had done some time). But he was not charged with murder. The accidental firing of Rick's gun left a bullet in the floor; this was enough evidence to support the lie Thomas had told: that Rick had fired first and Thomas was acting in self-defense.

There were two fights with Thomas that stand out for me. One showed me that I was capable of killing someone and the other showed me that I could be killed; both lifted Thomas' abuse of me to new heights. In the first one, I had been angry at Thomas for being gone all day. He came home high and I followed him into our back bedroom where the fight began. We moved all through the house arguing, until we ended up out on the front porch. Thomas' siblings were escalating the argument, when Thomas grabbed me and put me in a headlock. Through a very strained voice I told him that he was choking me. He thought that was funny and wouldn't let go. I started to panic, believing that he was going to kill me. I reached in my pocket and pulled out a multi-tool fingernail clipper I'd been using when he had come home a little earlier. Releasing a two-inch, pointy attachment, I jabbed it as hard as I could into Thomas' side. He was shocked that I had stabbed him and he became more enraged. But when he tried to speak no words came out. A look of panic came over his face, and he was having difficulty breathing when he collapsed to the porch floor. I ran into the house, afraid that any moment he would get his breath and come after me.

When he didn't chase me, I stumbled back outside to see the next few minutes unfold in slow motion. Everyone was panicking. Someone called 911 and Thomas was taken away in an ambulance. Apparently, when I stabbed him the nail file tool was just long enough to collapse one of his lungs. Thomas recovered but the love-hate line in our relationship had been crossed. The next fight would be a matter of survival, him or me. No matter how nice and loving his stories were, no matter how much I believed he loved me, I knew I had crossed the line and I knew he would want to get even. I tried to not fight back as much after that.

The second time we fought like that really was the last time. I think we argued about one of his girlfriends that he had been sneaking across the alley to see. This had been going on for months and I told him that I was sick of it. Thomas grabbed me right in the middle of my rant but I was able to pull away just as he was trying to punch me. I screamed and ran into our bedroom in the house. His mom, brother, and sister were just watching the fight escalate. Thomas chased me inside and I saw that look in his eyes: he had plans to do more than just slap me around. I felt in my bones that this time I was in danger of losing my life. Feeling trapped in the room with no way out, I threw myself at the closed window and when the glass broke I ended up falling out onto the front porch. Thomas followed me through the window, grabbed me from behind, and put me in a headlock with a knife against my throat. Taunting me, he said, "I'm gonna cut your throat." Just then, his brother Charles did something that he never had done before. He grabbed Thomas and pulled him off of me, telling Thomas that he was not going to let him kill me.

Then it all started to come back to me: why I tried to kill myself, how I had gotten here. I had completely forgotten who I was. I had forgotten how my mama had raised me. I had allowed Thomas to take away my dignity, my self-esteem, and I had been reduced to nothing. He had held my suicide attempt over my head, never letting me forget that he had been the one to call 911 the night I took all the pills and drank the booze. What I had not realized until that night was that as long as I was with him I was dead. I thought about God, and how this time I would not return. I knew that this was my chance to escape from all the madness. All of this ran through my head as I grabbed my baby, a few belongings, and left in a cab.

I gave the driver the address and he dropped us off a few blocks away at my sister Deborah's apartment building. We waited on the steps until Deb arrived home from work. I felt far removed from Thomas, and safer as time went by. *Did he really try to kill me just a few hours ago?* Deborah was surprised and happy to see us, but also concerned. Her apartment was clean and homey. I tried not to cry as I told her that I had left Thomas for good and that I didn't have anywhere else to go.

The day after finding refuge with my sister after my near-fatal fight with Thomas, I started the slow process of putting my life back together. This involved calling the welfare office to have my address changed and making arrangements with Dorothy to get our stuff out of her house. A month later, an apartment became available upstairs from my sister's place. Eventually, I would enroll in community college to begin collecting credits for an associate degree. I felt like a free woman. I could not believe it when Tamiko and I finally moved into our own place.

I never saw Thomas again after the day he tried to kill me. Over the years, I did run into his sisters. I was always amazed to hear them talk to me as if nothing had happened.

"Why don't you visit us," they would say. "You know Tamiko is still a part of the family. She needs to know her cousins, Brenda," they would say. I would just play it off and change the subject. Each time I saw them over the years, they looked worse than before. The last time that I saw Yvette, she was begging for money in front of a liquor store. She told me that Thomas was running a dope house and that he had his arm shot off by someone trying to rob his dope house. That time I made sure I was not being followed when I left them, I did not want them to know where I lived.

WASH, RINSE, REPEAT

I met Steve through my cousin, Linda. It had been quite a while since I had heard from her, having lost touch during the Thomas years. She called and said she wanted to see me, and to meet my baby Tamiko. Of course I wanted to see her. That's what Mama would have wanted: for us to stay in touch with the only family that we knew from her side. I got Tamiko ready for the visit and cleaned up the apartment. But instead of Linda coming to the door herself, she sent up her latest boyfriend, Ronnie. We went down to Linda's waiting car and I got in the back seat with Tamiko, right next to a dark-skinned, fine-looking man that Linda introduced as Steve, Ronnie's brother. Linda was still the same after all these years, still cracking "jokes" at my expense. She even recounted to the brothers in the car how I'd lost my virginity to a man just out of prison, not even recognizing that I had been raped. We rode around that day drinking beer and wine.

Later, Tamiko and I got into Steve's car and drove around with him. He impressed me with his nice shoes, his smoothness, his car; and he was kind to me. Steve was eleven years older than I was. This was really the first "date" I'd ever been on. When he took me back to my apartment, we kissed. Then he told me he was married and he left.

The next day, Steve came over again. Tamiko was very shy and reserved at first around Steve. She learned to like him though. He always made her laugh by grabbing on her toes and making his ears wiggle and making funny faces. I had just opened up the storage bin that retracted from the wall to see if any of the potatoes that I stored there were good enough to eat. The apartment had roaches. When he noticed the roaches in my potato bin, he didn't say anything except, "Would you like to go out to breakfast?" I liked how he didn't say what was obvious: that I had no food in the house. I liked how he made my baby laugh. I liked his confidence and the compact way he carried himself. We got in his car and listened to R&B music from the tape deck and I thought that this must be what it felt like to be taken care of. I tried to remain cool like I had experienced being cared for by a man before, like this was what usually happened and that going out to breakfast was what I expected. We ordered food to go.

Then driving back to my apartment, Steve cursed under his breath. I saw the flashing lights of a Detroit police car behind us. We were being pulled over. Steve quickly explained to me that he owed tickets and if they took him downtown, I should drive his car back to my apartment. He was handcuffed and placed in the back of the police car. I would soon learn that these encounters with the police were very frequent and I would make excuses for Steve. It would be years before I saw how this was all of his own making.

I didn't see Steve again until the next weekend when he invited Tamiko and me to a family picnic. I knew Steve was married but he told me that he was separated, and I believed him. What I learned at the picnic was that he still lived with his wife and five children. They admonished him for bringing me to the family event with his wife and children. I immediately felt ashamed for being there. Needless to say, we didn't stay long at this disaster of a picnic.

A few weeks later Steve moved in with us.

At the beginning, things were good. Steve was supportive of me taking classes at the community college, and loved to tell his buddies how smart I was. We worked hard to make a home out of the bottom half of a duplex we moved into together in a nice, safe neighborhood on Ashland Street with more white people than black people. Soon I was pregnant with his child. Steve was on disability from the railroad but had various part-time jobs; I was receiving welfare and food stamps. I had a partner who loved me as well as Tamiko. He was a good father and spoiled me rotten during my pregnancy. There were times when his two daughters would visit. They loved their father and treated me with respect. Steve was a very friendly and likable guy. I gave birth to our first baby together, a sweet girl named Michaell (pronounced, "Michelle"), which I spelled similar to my brother's name to honor the way he had always loved, protected, and cared for me. Steve also drank like I did. There were no physical fights yet; those came later.

Right away Steve began to pressure me about marriage. I did not want to get married to Steve or to anyone. I was afraid of being tied down. It also crossed my mind that because he had left his wife and kids, it was very possible that he would do the same to me. So we settled into a routine: drinking, fighting, and tearing each other down. Sometimes I thought I should slow down with my drinking. But I loved attention and fighting was one way for me to get it. I felt in my heart that marrying Steve was a mistake. But I kept thinking how much my children loved Steve and how he came into our life when I needed someone to love. I thought about how hard he hustled to help put food on the table. He was a good man at heart. So I finally agreed to marry him. Like most girls, I had always envisioned a fairy tale wedding with a white knight in shining armor to whisk me off to our castle. What I most remember about the day I married Steve is getting myself and the kids dressed, and getting drunk. I wore a white dress with red roses and green stems on it. We started drinking early that morning and then drove to the Coleman Young City-County Building in Detroit. In a large courtroom filled with other couples, a clerk delivered a speech. Then we all said in unison, "I do." That was it. I was so drunk I don't remember the drive home. And just like that it was over. We were married and life went back to the way it was.

Our children watched and listened to the increasing fights and were damaged by them. Take a love that was created when one man left an intact family to try to start another family. Add a woman who only knew abuse and abandonment. This was a recipe for disaster. I did not know how to be a wife. I only knew how to survive, how to get by. We were both too selfish to invest ourselves fully in this marriage. But we thought we were doing what was right. It might've worked if not for our history and our alcohol abuse. Even though we had a volatile relationship, I felt that this was as close as I was going to get to love. Steve told me many times that there was no one who would love me as much as he did, and I believed him. I also believed that I did not have anything to offer. I had three kids, I drank a lot, and I was on welfare. What knight was going to come rescue that?

ALL OF MY CHILDREN

Tamiko was three years old when Michaell was born. Michaell was different than Tamiko was as a baby. My second daughter was a healthy, fat, and happy baby. Soon though, I found out I was pregnant again. I was surprised. I was getting pregnant too fast for my body and mind to recover. My family was shocked too. Of course, Steve was happy when he heard the news. We both wanted a son and we both felt that I was pregnant with a boy.

I started experiencing pain that was not like anything I had felt with my other two pregnancies. I knew that there was something wrong. I also knew that this would be my last baby. The bigger my belly grew, the more intense my pain. I explained these feelings to the obstetrician, but the examinations and blood tests always came back normal. When I went into uncharacteristically excruciating labor and the baby's heartbeat began rapidly dropping, the doctors performed an emergency cesarean section. Michaell had been born by C-section and she turned out perfectly fine. Aaron Emanuel was born a healthy boy just before the umbilical cord that was wrapped around his neck did any damage. My son had a head full of coal black hair just as Tamiko and Michaell had. He was a carbon copy of Michaell as a baby and many people commented that they looked like twins. Holding my baby boy brought back all the previous feelings I had when Tamiko and Michaell were each born. I felt that it was my job to protect him. We also shared a unique and special bond because we had both been so close to death during my labor.

Michaell was only a little bit jealous when we brought Aaron home.

She was the middle child. Our dining room served as the bedroom. We had the sofa bed, a bassinet, and a baby crib in there. Michaell and Tamiko loved Aaron right away. They kissed him on his cheeks so much that his little face got chapped. Of course, Michaell wanted attention because she was the baby before Aaron and she was only two years old when he was born. Michaell would often climb in the baby crib and lie down. I had to continually get her out. Eventually she got used to the idea.

Michaell was a quiet little girl but she also had a curiosity that would get her into trouble. She was very mechanical-oriented. Michaell liked to see cause and effect. "What would happen if (fill in the blank)?" Drawing on the walls was one of her favorite pastimes; Michaell created most of the wall art in their bedroom. Then, when her brother got old enough, Michaell taught Aaron how to experiment in wall art, as well as other ways to get my attention. I repeatedly washed and scrubbed off the bedroom and living room walls. Over the course of a few years, we repainted these rooms several times, too.

I tried to settle into the role of "mother." It started out well. Steve even had longer periods of work that brought in enough money for once. So we were not too strapped for cash. The food stamps and welfare checks were the real lifesaver. Michaell and Tamiko treated Aaron like a little doll more than a little brother. The girls would prove to be a big help with their little brother. But I was overwhelmed. It was hard for me to consistently give love and attention to all three of my babies. I was beginning to snap at Michaell more and more. She received the brunt of my anger due to my stress.

Aaron was born in February and by that summer I was back to drinking moderately heavy. Right after I recuperated from childbirth, Steve and I returned to intimacy and I soon got pregnant again. I was devastated. I knew there was no way I could go through that again. I was very afraid. What if I died? What if the baby died? It had been such a hard time with the last pregnancy and birth. I told myself I just couldn't handle four kids. I was 24 years old. My body and my mind could not take it. Once I decided, I had to get up the nerve to have an abortion. I believed God knew my heart. But if He didn't understand,

He would forgive me. I wondered, though, if could I forgive myself for what I was about to do. I still had memories of the abortion I had in 1979 after I got pregnant with a second child by Thomas. It took years of drinking and crying to try to drown out those painful memories. When they would creep up, I would push them so far down that I thought they would never come out. Little did I know that these types of painful memories eventually burst out like an eruption. They beg for and deserve a proper grieving. My mind and my body would eventually be allowed to grieve these babies' deaths in time. And though I still felt the pain of grief, I knew that first abortion had been necessary in order to prevent another child from living with the pain of sickle cell disease that Tamiko suffered everyday.

Everything in my life seemed to be a struggle. I tried to get my tubes tied, and even that was difficult. So, of course, I got angry. St. John's didn't believe in birth control or abortion. I decided that because it was my body and that I would be the one responsible for any more children, I would go to a non-Catholic hospital. Here was another time that my Catholic faith would disappoint me. Eventually I went to another hospital. After the tubal ligation, I felt that I had taken a stand. I wondered how many other young women at St. John's Hospital were turned down? How many women like me who really respected the medical field, had been given no choice about birth control.

The Detroit Park system had a program in those parks and the majority of the children who attended were from low-income families. The park system would provide a free lunch to children and their parents. My kids loved this. For me, it was a godsend because I didn't have to worry about lunch. Sometimes it was breakfast for my kids if we got up late, or if we didn't have any breakfast. When we did have it, breakfast consisted of cream of wheat, cold cereal, grits, or oatmeal, and toast. We also received food from the Focus Hope Supplemental Food Program. This program gave infant milk, dried eggs, powdered milk, block cheese, and canned meats to mothers with small children. We ate pretty well if it was the time of the month when food stamps had been picked up. This would usually only last for half of the month, and even then we were always scrambling to buy tissue and diapers.

So during the summertime, we would walk to the park six or seven blocks away. It was where I went to watch my kids play. I spent a lot of time comparing their life to other kids'. We were near the bottom of the stack in this comparison, but there were always kids who were worse off. Infrequently, I would go to the park's outdoor community pool to cool off. But I was always afraid of the possibility of trouble. Fights and shootings could break out over trivial things.

Of my three children, I always kept a closer eye on Tamiko, making sure that she did not get too cold—a trigger for a sickle cell attack. I felt that I should get as much help as was available to help Tamiko with this disease, though we knew that there was not a lot of information out there. Later, I wrote a research paper for one of my college English classes on sickle cell and my daughter. I was amazed to find out that even the library did not have much information. What I did find chronicled the disease from Africa to the Americas and Europe. The only documentation relayed the most extreme results of the disease including malformed extremities and cysts. This was so extreme and shocking that I never told my family, especially Tamiko, what my research uncovered. Doctors told me that Tamiko would not live past five years of age and she had proven them wrong.

During medical visits, the doctors not only evaluated Tamiko; they also evaluated me as a parent. The idea was to see how I managed as a parent of a child with sickle cell. I sat with a psychologist who questioned me about my ability to deal with this situation. She talked to me about not treating Tamiko different from my other kids. She knew from experience with other families that we tended not to discipline sickle cell children for fear that getting too upset would trigger a crisis. We kept them out of most activities for fear of a crisis. No playing in the hot sun or cold snow. Most families' entire lives revolved around their sickle cell children. From the beginning of the conversation, my shame returned. I told this doctor how guilty I already felt to have given

Tamiko this painful disease, and that there was no way I was going to discipline her by spanking as I did Michaell and Aaron. The doctor told me that if I didn't discipline Tamiko she'd become spoiled rotten and unable to adjust to life when she got older. She enrolled Tamiko in the new sickle cell clinic at Detroit Children's Hospital. This meant regular visits with specialists, great preventative care, orthopedic treatments, and great advice on how to avoid a full-blown sickle cell crisis.

At the end of one of these visits, the doctor asked me a question. "What do you do to relieve your stress? You work, have three children, one with a terminal disease, and you just completed school. How do you relax?" And before I could stop the answer from coming out of my mouth, I looked the doctor squarely in the eye and told her I drink. She was not shocked. In fact, she seemed to already know that. I tried to clean it up and backpedal by explaining. I told her about taking a hot bath and having a glass of wine in the tub. But we both knew that this was a watered-down version of the truth: I drank often and I drank heavily.

My father and mother out for a drink with his two sisters from Philly

Mike, Ms. Mary and Tamiko at one of the many
family get togethers at Ms. Mary's house.

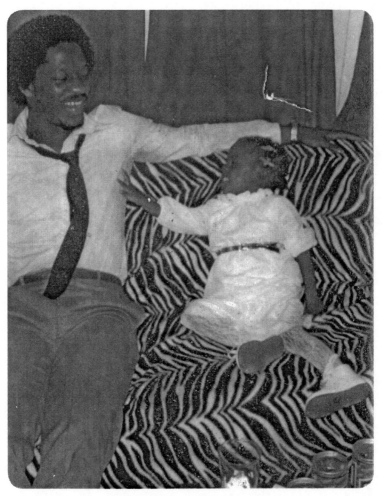

Mike playing with Tamiko

Pushing Tamiko in our first apartment on Charlevoix

Michaell, Tamiko, Aaron and cousin Sierra on Eastlawn

Brenda in the Garden on Parkgrove

Brenda in front of house on Parkgrove

Michaell, Tamiko, and Aaron with Sandy, the stray dog
rescued from an abandoned house next door on Parkgrove

Lansing, Michigan – 1999 Mother's Day visit

The experience of a lifetime: me on top of
the world at Everest basecamp 2014

INSTITUTIONS, CHURCH

I continued to take a few classes at the community college. I found that school was something that I did well. I liked the rewards of getting the grades, as well as the competition in class. This was my way to stand out, to be recognized for something. Part of my financial aid package included work-study so I got a job in the student computer lab. Just like that, I found my niche. Working in the computer lab and going to college gave me purpose. Here were two things I could do, and do very well.

I loved computers. I was one of six technicians who helped to run the lab. I would lose myself in green screens and green bar paper. The logic of code helped me feel safe and secure. Things could only be one way or the program would not run. I loved debugging a program. I felt like a detective, looking through the code to find out what was preventing a job from running.

We started with simple programs to those with hundreds of lines of code. Complicated loops and go-to routines inside of other routines; I loved it. I would bring homework to the house, get a glass of wine or beer, and debug into the wee hours. I really felt that the booze helped my mind to comprehend the complexities of computer language. At least, that was my excuse. It wasn't long before I was done with all of my computer classes. It was not long either before I got in trouble at school for my drinking.

Back on Ashland the neighborhood had changed. Steve and I had

91

an opportunity to move to the upstairs flat which was much nicer and seemingly safer. Steve worked nights and I would be home alone with the kids. A young mother and her twelve-year-old son moved into our old downstairs flat. The mother was nice, and quiet. She worked during the day most of the time. Her son was also nice.

One night after they had moved in, we heard loud noises coming from downstairs. There were screams that were followed by loud whacks, as if a belt was being used to hit something or someone. We could hear the boy crying. At first we just thought that the son was being disciplined. But we suddenly realized that the mother's guy friend was down there. He must have had the little boy tied up in the basement and he was beating him trying to find out where the mother was. We could hear the boy begging for the guy to stop. Steve picked up the phone and dialed 911. I lay there terrified. Around fifteen minutes later the police showed up. We knew the police were going to question us, but I nearly jumped out of my skin when I heard the police knock on our door. We answered their questions and asked a few of our own. We were told the boy was okay and had been taken to the hospital. After the suspect was captured, he began writing letters to me from jail. He knew that we had called the police and talked in detail about coming to get me. I became frightened that once he was released he would kill me. I began to have nightmares about this.

This series of events and my increased drinking contributed to full-blown fear and paranoia. I was always watching my back and was afraid to answer the phone. I was not doing very well with my algebra and computer classes. I cried a lot. I would not move away, even though I was terrified. Then I began to hear voices and was really losing touch with reality. There were times when I would zone out. I began to sit and just stare at nothing. Sometimes I just did not want to get out of bed, and when I did I just went through the motions. School was no longer my refuge. It became harder and harder to concentrate. I was tired and listless.

I had heard that there were people who would go to the hospital for a short period to get a rest from all of the problems in their lives. This is what I had seen from all of my years of staying at home during the day and going to school at night. I would watch the soap operas on television.

So I thought that this was what I needed. I was just tired and there were too many things going on in my life. I had three small children under the age of five. It was hard, and my life was stressful with this criminal living downstairs. Who wouldn't need a rest? So I got out the Yellow Pages, found the Wayne County Mental Hospital in downtown Detroit, and called for an appointment.

When I arrived there a week later I had no idea what I was doing. I remember Steve and the kids coming with me. I was allowed in but they were not. I remember waving goodbye to them. Once inside I could see them through the grated windows. I continue to wave as I walked through the door. I was escorted through an inner door by a guy in a white coat; I heard the lock engage as the last door closed. I knew that this had been a mistake. I thought everything would work out once I got to see the doctor, got evaluated and explained that I was just there for a rest.

I had dressed very nice, like I would for any doctor appointment. A week earlier in an attempt to bring me out of my depression, Steve had bought me a pair of knee length black leather boots. They were expensive for us, but he knew that they would cheer me up for a bit. Later, somebody in the institution stole those brand new boots and my cigarettes.

I decided that I must've picked the wrong hospital. I was not crazy. I just needed to rest. A two-or three-day stay was what I was hoping for. But they had given me medicine and I suddenly found it difficult to talk; the words that I heard in my head somehow were not coming out of my mouth. The doctor told me that I was suffering from depression and that I needed further evaluation. I began to feel threatened. I asked if I could leave when I felt ready to go home. He told me he could not allow that. It seemed like by signing myself in, I had given up all my rights to judge my own competence. The doctor was the only one who could release me. I got scared. What the hell had I done? I couldn't stay there forever; I had kids, school, and shit to do. I only wanted a break. I was so afraid that I would flunk school and lose my tuition money.

The next day as I got ready for school I had a thought. What would stop me from just taking off, once they let me out? I could catch a bus and go home. What could they do? The nurse looked at me as if she knew what I was thinking. She began to explain the policy around being let out on a day pass. There was a maximum-security mental hospital in Ypsilanti, Eloise, and that is where they housed the criminally insane people. Folks never get out. Shock treatment and straight-jackets were the norm. That's where a person was sent if they ran off but got caught. I went to school and came right back.

After a few days of not taking the pills, I began to return to normal. It was ironic that the pills made me feel crazy. I wondered what they made crazy people feel like.

Although I was still crazed with fear, I realized something: God could help me with my crazy feelings. So I started going to church almost every Sunday. I would walk the eight or nine blocks to a small church near Jefferson Avenue. Every time I went, I was hung over from drinking Friday and Saturday nights. I tried to remember what I had heard as a child in church. This was all mixed in with information I had gathered over the years. It was like I had a life dresser and one of the drawers had church stuff. I remembered how God had helped others. I saw where Miss Wilson from my childhood had believed that God watched over her and her children. I knew from my own experience that God had helped Mike and me after Mama died. But I was so conflicted. I was still blaming God for taking my mother. But I also began to see that most of the hardship was not God. It was what men did to other men. I listened to the preacher every Sunday from ten to noon, and after every service I would leave church feeling sad because I thought it was not helping me.

I would go to the beer store across from the church and buy tall cans of brew to drink on the way home. There I was dressed up in church clothes, drinking a can of beer, wondering why God was not working in my life. I believed in God but I stopped believing in preachers. I could still pray but I did not need church to do it. Never once did I think drinking had anything to do with my problem. I thought I might drink a bit too much sometimes, but I was in control and I could stop if I wanted to. I stopped attending church. My life continued to be chaotic. I continued drinking heavily.

Steve and I fought all of the time. The fights began to escalate from verbal to physical. We would fight and reconcile, and repeat. When I wasn't fighting with Steve, I fought with the neighbors. Arguments with my neighbors were common. I was a tyrant in my neighborhood. I was small but loud. I would have a few drinks, turn my stereo up full blast, and dare anyone to ask me to turn it down. School is what fed me and it was my head that grew. I knew that I was better than a lot of my neighbors. Better than everyone I came in contact with in my neighborhood, in fact. I believed that with my brainpower I floated above everyone.

I began to think about what would happen to me after I graduated with my Associates Degree. I fantasized about being able to get a high paying job. I looked at the potential for full- time employment in a business office. I had always wanted to work in an office, to dress for business every day and work from nine to five like business people. This was my dream. I could then fulfill my mother's dream of getting myself and my kids out of the ghetto so that we had a chance of making it.

I had survived, up until then, on sheer willpower. I was stuck between being a good girl and being a sinner. I still longed for help. I still had hope and faith that God could take care of me if I just kept being a good girl. But it was hard. I would drink and the bad girl would come out.

I finished school and I fell into a big depression. The instant gratification of getting grades and being on the dean's list was over. I tried to hold on to the specialness I got from school as long as I could. But I was back to being not special, just another person in the hood. Nobody cared about my specialness. Nobody cared that I had graduated summa cum laude, with a 4.0 grade point average, and had an Associate's of Applied Science Degree in Computer Science.

I went home the day of graduation thinking about Mama and how proud she would have been. It took ten years to get my degree. What was I going to do to make that time pay off? I was still on welfare, still living in the ghetto. Mama would want me to continue on with my education. I was the first in my family to ever complete a degree.

DADDY

teve and I would visit my dad and Ms. Mary on the west side of Detroit. Daddy was a full-blown alcoholic by that time. Mrs. Mary and Daddy had finally gotten married, and Mike and I had been there for the wedding. Deborah and Junior were not interested in attending; they had not forgiven our dad yet. I loved my daddy and would go over to their house a lot. I loved Ms. Mary also. Though there were times when we would drive to pick up Daddy from his girlfriend's house and we would drink over there with daddy and his Ms. Sally. Other times Daddy would walk home drunk, and he became a target for muggings by young boys.

Mostly for holidays, we would meet over at Ms. Mary's house for the family dinner. These get-togethers were always filled with food, drinking, card games, and laughter; they always ended in fighting. We would play bid whisk and spades. The drinking would reach a fever pitch. And then it would only take one statement. Daddy would usually fight with Deborah or Junior, less often with Mike or me. Alcohol was always running the show and directing the arguments. We would get enraged, drink a little more, and storm out, only to return on the next invitation from Ms. Mary.

What a crazy time that was. I loved my family. We all had our positions, our roles in the pecking order. I was the baby of the family, the screw-up. I had tried to commit suicide. I had three children out of wedlock: one child whose father was a heroin addict and the other who had left his five children to father another child out of wedlock. Mike was the baby boy who didn't finish high school, who may not have even been my father's child. Deborah was the independent girl who had worked since high school. Junior was the accomplished one who had been in the Air Force, traveling to foreign places.

And Daddy was a drunk who I looked up to. I wanted validation from all of them. So I continued to visit, I continued to try to be the good child. I would visit when no one else would. I could be bribed to go over. The promise of food for the kids—because sometimes we had none—sweetened with the free booze, would be just enough enticement to get us over there.

Daddy was strange around the kids. He never really seemed like he enjoyed them. Maybe he did, but I think he tolerated them instead. I tried to give my kids everything I could. During one particular visit when I was appeasing my daughter by letting her grunt for what she wanted rather than having her ask for it directly, Daddy looked me square in the eye. He said, "You ain't gon' ever have anything in this life." I was shocked and startled. I looked at him dumbfounded. I managed to ask him why.

He continued, "Because you will give everything you have to them damn kids!" It was like a stinging slap in the face, and it confused me.

"Why wouldn't I give everything I have to my kids? That's what parents are supposed to do! That's why your kids hate you, because you never gave us anything." I never forgot what he said. It would be years down the line before I understood that he was correct. My children would need to learn how to stand on their own two feet. I would only hamper their growth by providing for them all of the time.

EMPLOYMENT

B y the time I was thirty years old, I had three children and had been on welfare my entire life. When I was born, my mom was on welfare and I was added to her case. My children were added the same way. I had gone to school to try to break the cycle and as a way to have some victory and satisfaction in my life. So when I walked into the Department of Social Services office that cold winter morning, hands full of the receipts, bills, and other paperwork I'd inevitably need, I thought it would be a routine review. I did not see that a huge change was about to happen, a change that would be responsible for turning my life in a new direction. My (social) "worker" looked over the papers and seemed to feel like I did, that everything was in order.

We began to talk and she asked me what were my plans upon graduation. I told her, thinking that this was the right answer, that I wanted to continue on to get my Bachelor's degree in computer science. She launched into a monologue about the State's plan to help welfare mothers enter the workforce; they felt like it was time for me to get a job. I told her that I didn't think I could get a job in computers until I had a Bachelor's. She told me that I didn't have to get a computer job; I had to get a *paying* job. I became distraught. I didn't want just any job; I wanted a good job so I could get off welfare. The only job I felt I could get at this time was flipping burgers. I felt the anger boiling up inside of me. They were going to ruin it all. I had a four-year plan and they were going to cut me short of my dream. Sweat was beading up in the middle of my back, trickling down my shoulder blades. I wished I had a drink. I had to get hold of myself before I said something I would regret. I took a deep breath and repeated that I would not flip burgers and if the State of Michigan wanted me to work, they would need to help find me a good job.

The social worker told me she was recommending me for a new program designed to take welfare recipients off of the State's payroll and put them to work. This program would continue to provide all the benefits I was already getting plus a five dollar an hour stipend for the work I would do. This would continue until I received enough raises to not need the welfare program any longer. I would also get a small stipend to purchase a few office work clothes from the Goodwill resale shop. I was stunned and speechless, so she continued. This program would have me work right there in the welfare office as an office clerk, filing and supporting the social workers. I think at that point I had to pick my jaw up off the floor. If I needed help with childcare, that too would be provided.

Most of what she said had me in a state of shock. She was not sure about all of the details like when I would start or if I even met all of the program requirements. But one thing she was sure of was that the State of Michigan and I were embarking on a new relationship. I felt like the State of Michigan was pushing me out of a tree. They were not easing me into this, just a swift kick out into the world. Fall or fly.

When I left to get the bus home, I was in a daze. I had a huge pack of papers that explained the new Job Start program. I did not understand most of what was happening, but I felt that it would be temporary until I got my résumé out and all of the major businesses would see my 4.0 GPA and Dean's list for four years straight and they would be scrambling among themselves to hire me. I thought I just had to get myself out there. Surely, one of the computer companies would want a smart girl like me. IBM or Burroughs Corporation. The companies that I saw on television where folks wore suits to work and sat around a water cooler. Yes, I would get my own job.

When I got home, I sat drinking and talking about this to Steve. I drank so that I could think clearly. What was I going to do? I had to do what they said or get a job on my own. Steve said maybe I was looking at it the wrong way. It could be a chance to work starting at the bottom and working my way up. He could not wait to tell his mother and friends that I was going to work at the welfare office. Steve supported the idea. We agreed that Steve would care for the kids if I got chosen. Aaron was six years old, Michaell was eight, and Tamiko was eleven. I remember how good I felt telling my children that mommy was going to work. I finally felt like a real person. There would be times I know that Steve would regret so wholeheartedly supporting me in this endeavor, as the job ended up separating us. This new path would cause me to feel more elite and would increase my ego.

Over the next few weeks I had many appointments at the welfare office. I was also assigned a job coach. The truth was: I was terrified. I did not know how to be at work. I never knew how to be around people who were not like me. Back then I had no self-esteem. In my neighborhood and in my mind, I was a queen. In my school I knew where I stood; I was a 4.0- dean's-list student. But where did I fit in this new world of work? This new adventure was not being looked at as an opportunity for growth and expansion into the world of work. The people who surrounded me looked at this as another short-term project dreamed up by the welfare system to give me a low-paying job and to keep an eye on me. There were six of us who were chosen to continue through the program. Later, there would be competition among the six of us to become permanent employees.

Entering the building in those first weeks of the job, I overheard one of the female employees remark in a snide tone, "Oh, they just let anybody work here now. They just picking people up off the streets." Whose bright idea was this to put me to work with the same people who had all of the details of my life in a folder? I would have preferred to work in an office where the folks did not already know me. They would have had less chance of looking down on me.

I had something that these workers did not know about. As we were growing up, Mama would instill pride in us by telling us that we were Joneses. That Joneses don't quit. This meant that we were strong people. I knew this new job opportunity would be the time to act like I was just as good as my coworkers were. So I began to watch them. I paid close attention to how they behaved, how they walked and talked.

I remember one of the trainers telling us that we had to dress for and act like the position we wanted to have. So I straightened my shoulders, held my head up high, and every day I walked into that office with those thoughts in my head. There were those who gave me grief, and there were so many others who went out of their way to help me.

I had faith that this would be okay. My faith had been made stronger by believing this job had to be orchestrated by God in order to give my kids and me the chance to make it in this world. With all of the schooling, all of the beatings, the loss of my mama, and all of the other really bad stuff, I felt that God was looking at me. Maybe with the urging of my mother's spirit, God was saying, "Okay, let's give her a shot." Who was I to screw it up? This was bigger than I was. I had to give it my all.

I felt strange every time I walked into the building and passed the clients waiting in the lobby. I could feel the same resentment coming from the clients as I used to have toward the workers. Every discomfort that I experienced came from knowing how they felt about me. I was now a worker. A clerical worker not a social worker, but we all looked the same to them. All of the anger about life's unfairness—from shut-off notices to food stamp reductions—was now directed at me. I knew because I had felt that same way. I felt bad that I got to work and that my life might be getting better yet so many still had to come here for help. I would grapple with this guilt for some time.

In the break room in the back, my coworkers talked about vacations and where they went for the weekend. They shared details about how their children were doing in college. I couldn't relate to any of it. In fact, it made me feel ashamed. I felt that I had nothing to offer to that kind of conversation. I did become friends with some of the other clerical workers. They were happy to see me because there was a lot of work to do. Mostly, we helped out with filing cases. It was at this time I began to develop my work ethic. I had to work hard so that I could show people that I was a good worker. I wanted people to notice me, to compliment me, to validate me. I wanted the other employees to know that I was competent. I continued being "the good girl" in this way. So, I worked hard and always went the extra mile.

But, there were times when I went to work hung over. There were times when I had bruises on me, or my eyes had broken blood vessels because of fights with Steve. It was hard to hide the fact that I had issues with both my man and with drinking.

Something told me that this was my way out, my chance to finally have a reasonably good life. But first I had to become a permanent employee. Then, one day I got my break. Sally, one of the most senior of the permanent, full-time clerical workers, did not come in to work. She had called in sick. This continued for weeks. I was asked to help with her duties. Weeks turned into months. I heard the talk in the smoke room and in the coffee area. Sally had stopped calling in sick. She had stopped calling in at all. Eventually, I found out that Sally drank and she had decided not to come back to work. Her coworkers and boss were worried about her; they wanted Sally to go through the proper procedures so that she could retire and get her benefits from the State of Michigan. No one could figure out why she would not do this. But, about five years later, I would personally understand why Sally wouldn't do what made sense, to collect her benefits. She had given up on life. A month later, they found her dead in her home; she drank herself to death. That's how I got hired for a permanent position with the State of Michigan.

NEIGHBORHOOD, BUS STOPS & FIRE

I worked full-time. The kids were doing the best that they could. Steve seemed to be hanging out with more shady people. And then the neighborhood started changing.

Bus stops became terrifying for me; things happened there that seemed unimaginable and crazy. People were shot in drive-by shootings; women and little girls were raped. People were robbed and beaten. Detroit was the murder capital of the U.S., and all of the news that I heard had a drastic effect on me. My bus stop was in front of a large liquor store and all kinds of people - dealers, women of the night, winos - hung out or stopped there. I often thought of walking the couple of blocks to the next bus stop but that made me a lone target. I thought it might be better to be in a group of other people who were waiting for the bus instead of being by myself. I walked to the stop by myself at 6:00 in the morning most days. Folks still up from last night's party or drug deals were still out. This was the time of morning when wild dogs roamed the streets in packs. People asked me if I had a cigarette and I would put on my brave don't-mess-with-me face, my bad-ass-I'll-pull-out-my-9-millimeter-gun-and-light-you-up-if-you-get-crazy attitude, my watch-out-for-the-cans-of-whoop-ass in my raggedy purse stance. Tough on the outside melted butter on the inside. I was afraid of everything. I would give the desolate soul a square (cigarette) and would feel some safety. People had been beaten bloody for not sharing. Maybe he wouldn't hurt me if I shared: still thinking my "good girl" behavior could save me.

I don't know how many times I was singled out because I had on nice clothes and they could see that I had just came from the welfare office. I would get harassed. They would ask me why they did not get a check or why the check was late. They wanted to know why their worker never called them back or why she didn't even answer the phone. This, too, was scary. I would give them half-assed answers like, "Oh, your worker is Ms. Williams? She only answers her phone early in the morning. Try her at 7 AM." Eventually, the regulars who hung out there got used to seeing me, saw that I was just like them, and I was no longer hassled.

Crack was moving into the neighborhood and I thought it was time to move out. I saw a lot of Michael and Deborah around this time. Michael lived on the same street as I did and he was glad I was moving; so was he. By this time, Mike was drinking like a fish, getting into trouble, and losing jobs, and he and Deborah were not getting along either. Deborah had a baby by then and our kids played together quite a bit. She was glad I was moving and she, too, was thinking about doing so.

I remember when Steve found our new house. I had been at work and he had continued to hunt for a place while I was there. I got off work and we drove over to this nice white house. We could not go in but we peeked in the front and back windows. This was a nice house, two stories with a large front room and dining room. At that time we could not see the kitchen or the bedrooms. Steve made an appointment for us to see this house and a few days later we were walking around in it. I loved it. Aaron and the girls loved it. It was perfect. The front yard had a nice long porch with bushes for privacy. The neighborhood was nice and quiet and, again, mixed with black and white folks. People seemed to keep their yards up, cutting their grass and tending to flowers. I could walk to work. I told Steve that I wanted to see the area at night and on weekends to check out the prospective neighbors and to see if there would be loud music, fighting, drugs or drinking: all of the things that I was trying to leave behind. I absolutely did not know that that I was bringing my own mess with me. Though I did not have any credit, never having bought anything brand new before, I was able to get a bank loan. A house in my name! Once the deal was done we all grew a bit uppity.

I really did not have many friends at that time. I had gotten drunk and cussed out most of my old neighbors numerous times. But I did not know how much I was disliked until I received a phone call at work. Steve was frantic. Our old house was on fire! Rumors circulated saying that the fire department thought that it had been arson.

It just so happened that the night before the fire, just after sealing the house deal, we had decided to take some blankets and pillows to spend the night in the new house. We raced over to our old place and found total devastation. The entire back of the house was burned. I was in tears. All of our stuff was in there ruined: the kids' clothes, furniture, photos, food, everything.

Looking at this horror, I was reminded of the other tragedies by fire I had experienced: the couch fire started by Mama's cigarette when I was about four years old, and the garage fire when I was nine. I picked up a few damaged baby pictures of the kids and left in shock. We drove back to the new, empty house and sat there trying to comfort the kids. I tried to keep a strong face for them. The happiness that they felt from moving to this wonderful house was now replaced with fear. We got food to eat, and booze to drink away the pain. I remember thinking about how I felt, how my mother was my rock during the time we had the couch and garage fires. I remember thinking that my mother would keep me safe. But as soon as the children were asleep I broke down. I needed to be comforted: I reached for something to drink, and then I reached for Steve.

The next day a coworker came over to our new house with used clothes that have been donated. He also told me that the district manager of our new office had authorized him to write up a purchase order for a refrigerator, stove, washer, and dryer. I could not believe how nice everyone at work was being. So we tried to pull ourselves together and thank God that we were not in the old house when it caught on fire.

Within a two-to three-year period, the streets around our new house started to be plagued with crack and crack dealers. Crime shot up. Drive-by shootings, fire-bombings of homes, crack dens, and gang hangouts were increasing. There was a constant battle for turf. The neighborhood was at war and we found ourselves right in the middle of it. The streets that I thought were safe enough to walk at night became filled with new gangs of thugs. These were very young boys who found out that they could lead others by intimidation, humiliation, threats, and violence. These were young boys that my daughters and son knew who had been nice kids stopping by my house, calling me "Mrs. Fantroy," and eating in my home when I had cookouts. These boys found a sick, twisted, family structure in the gang life, one that they did not find at home.

Porch sitting used to be one of my favorite pastimes that I learned from my mother. Porch sitting kind of ran in my family. It's sitting and watching what is going on in the neighborhood, taking it all in. I've seen quite a bit from my front porch. But I never realized how that view was really a window out into what was going on in the larger world. I could not see past my small world. My view would get much larger once I got off the porch and into the world.

So there I was, chilling, when my eyes noticed a rundown black car turn onto our block. There were four black guys in it and they were driving very slowly. I got a sick feeling in my stomach. My intuition told me that somehow this was bad, very bad. I was too afraid or too nosy to move, but I did grab my beer as my body moved to the front door on its own.

Two houses down, a young neighbor boy was walking up his steps. As my hand grabbed the front door to go in, I heard the shots. One of the guys in the car had jumped out and shot my neighbor twice in the head. I ran inside and fell to the floor. I crawled through the house yelling for everyone to get down, that there was shooting outside. Time seemed to stand still as we crawled together on the floor of the front room. We could hear the car as it burned rubber and screeched off down the street.

I heard a bloodcurdling scream outside. We knew even in those early days that we did not want to be the one who could describe in detail what we'd seen. It was never safe to have witnessed any crime. No one was actually caught for this crime. The boy who was murdered was just one child in a long line of young black kids caught up in the war.

I had always dreamed of having enough room outside to build a garden. I loved to get up early in the morning and pick the weeds out of the garden. It got pretty cramped, as my crops grew. We cleared a patch of the yard close to the fence that separated us from the back alley. I even had a healthy garden-growing competition with my father. He would come over and if we were out back, which was where we barbecued before it got too bad, he would critique my garden. I learned a lot from him on these occasions. He would tell me not to plant too much, too close. I loved the feeling of the dirt in my fingers. I enjoyed watching the plants grow and showing the kids how you could get food from one little seed. The garden gave me so much pleasure, and peace. I would till my garden on the weekends, and then prepare a barbecue cookout. My gardening all came to an end when the alley became a pathway for shady characters. I would be in the yard working the soil and gang members would run through the alley, chasing or being chased. It was really creepy and I became too afraid to work out in my own garden.

When I was a kid growing up, I'd hear crickets as I sat on my porch in the summertime. We caught fireflies in glass jars and just thought they were the coolest thing. My own kids were not allowed out at night. The sounds that my children grew up with were of gunshots and sirens. There was not one night that went by when there was not a shootout.

The increasing crime affected my kids at school too. When Michaell was thirteen she experienced a horrific event at school. One day on her way into the building, a shootout started. Before she could run for cover, the gunman—a teenage boy—grabbed her, pulled out his gun, and used my baby girl as a shield. He began to shoot at a rival gang member with Michaell as his protection. Finally, he let her go and she ran into the school. She came home traumatized. After that, all three of my kids were afraid to go to school.

During one shootout, I called 911 on my phone. I told the operator that there was a shootout going on right outside my window, in the vacant lot next door. The operator was so professional she seemed almost detached. She asked me to describe what was going on. I told her that my kids and I were on the floor and that there was shooting outside. I put the phone close to the window so she could hear it for herself. She asked me if I knew who was doing the shooting. I told her I didn't. I reminded her that I was crouched on the floor with my kids and that we were scared to death. She asked if I could look out the window to see who was doing the shooting. Whispering to her, I said, "Lady, I'm not going to look out of that window. People are shooting out there. Can't you send someone?" She said she would. The police never came. I felt like the police and the city officials had actually abandoned the people who lived in the city and that they were really just waiting for the war to die down.

Another time, I witnessed a white guy being dragged out of his car as thugs rifled through his pockets. Then they started ransacking the car. Eventually the guy was left in the street and a group of thugs pushed his car away. They beat him and left him in the street and then stole the car. Nobody, including me, called the police. I'm not sure they would have come if we did. This was like the Wild West. We pretty much barricaded ourselves in the house and only went out during the day when we really had to. I was increasingly afraid of everything and everybody.

I was just going through the motions, working and coming home. It was normal for us to hit the floor every time we heard a shootout. We crawled around, making no noise. We felt like we were in a war zone, never knowing when a bullet could come through the window. Then the unthinkable happened.

Detroiters were well known for the devil's night Halloween ritual of torching abandoned houses. So much publicity was given to this that news crews from around the world would fly into Detroit each October 31 to cover that story. The city, in an effort to reduce the fires every October, would knock down the abandoned houses. But they never cut down the tall grass that grew in place of these houses. The grass was taller than most of the small children. We mothers often told our kids to stay out of the lots because we could not see them.

So I was sitting on the porch and the kids, mine and two others, came running up onto the porch out of breath. They told me that there was a dead body in the lot next to our house. I could not believe that. How? I had been sitting right there. I did not see or hear anything.

I got up and walked over to the lot. Sure enough the body of a woman, black, was in the field. She looked dead and her eyes were wide open. She was naked and looked like she had panties around her neck as if she had been strangled. Her arms were stretched out above her and there was a flattened grass trail below her feet. It was as if she had been dragged to this spot. I vividly remember seeing flies crawling on her lips. There was no blood. I ran back into the house and called 911. I told them that there was a body of a dead woman in the lot next door to my house. Within five minutes, people from all over came out and a large crowd formed to see the body. I kept my kids on the porch and then I told one of my children to get a blanket. Steve went to cover the woman up.

Some in the crowd were disappointed. We waited on the porch for the police. I was amazed and confused. How could this happen right there while I sat on my porch and we heard nothing unusual, saw no one? Aaron had ridden his bike through the lot numerous times during the day and he said he saw nothing.

When the police came we were questioned. Eventually, I got the feeling that the police did not believe us. How could we not have seen anything, they wondered? I was afraid that they thought Steve or I had something to do with this murder. Eventually I shut down. I knew that that would cast more suspicion my way. I explained to the police what we saw and then I told them that I was done with this. We did not know the woman and we did not see who put her there. Yes, we covered her up but not because we knew her, but because a crowd of people had gathered to stare at her.

I was very frustrated after they left. This was the final straw. I felt deep down in my heart that if I continue to live here something bad would happen to me or to my children. After the woman was found, I could not shake this feeling of doom. It was such a sad time for me. This was when my feelings of hopelessness really started.

ALCOHOLIC CRACK

I knew I was drinking too much. I didn't care. I was just following in my father's footsteps, except I would not end up like him. I would find a way to beat this thing when I needed to. Of course, I didn't need to yet. I did not know it at the time but this was the beginning of the six-year spiral into the depths of my drinking.

I was sick of my life, my choices, and myself. For the hundredth time I wanted my mama. I wanted someone to help take away the pain. There was no one, so I did the next best thing. I returned to alcohol. I never thought that I might be using alcohol to help me deal with my issues. Drinking was just something I did to calm myself or to relax. During the day I would get up in the morning feed the kids, wash them up and put on clean clothes and get myself ready for the day. They would play while I cleaned up the house. The cycle was continuous and the spiral was deep. I was trying to outrun myself. But there I was at every turn.

I blacked out on a sidewalk and split open the back of my head. At the hospital a doctor told me that I had suffered from an overdose of alcohol. I didn't believe a person could overdose on alcohol. The doctor would not let me go home until the alcohol had been flushed out of my system. So there I sat in that hospital just inside the boundary of one of the wealthiest neighborhoods in Michigan, with IV fluid slowly pushing through my veins until I was alcohol-diluted enough to be released. Just being there caused me to feel ashamed. I hated myself and I felt that every patient and employee in this all-white, rich hospital hated me and were repulsed by the drunken, dirty sight of me. I felt that this was an isolated experience. I had no idea that over the next ten years I would need to be taken to the emergency room many times due to overdosing on the amount of alcohol my system could take. My body was giving me warnings and I was not listening. I was petite, weighing about one hundred pounds. My mind told me that all I needed to do as moderate. Never once did I think of how frightened my children and Steve must have been. I wasn't afraid at all; I just needed to be more careful. These hospital visits did not stop me from drinking to celebrate, or drinking after a hard day at work, or drinking with friends, or just drinking to drink. Steve would tell me that I should slow down a bit and I agreed. So I would not drink hard liquor or wine during the week, only on weekends.

If I was drinking and Tamiko had a sickle cell crisis, I would often wait until morning or until the medicines that I had for her no longer worked. We both hated for her to be in the hospital. I am ashamed to admit my reasons, but mostly because of the inconvenience. Sitting at the hospital all night, taking off work, making sure Michaell and Aaron were okay, or taking them with me to sit at the hospital. But the biggest inconvenience was that Tamiko's extended hospital stays interfered with my drinking. And I used my drinking to try to forget the shame and guilt I felt for carrying the gene that gave my child this disease.

I also tried crack, even though I knew about and feared becoming addicted to it. One night at a friend's house, I drew and held in the smoke just like she said. I felt myself simultaneously drift away and become heightened. I thought to myself about how this might not be a good idea, but it was too late. I was off and running. The first night we finished up the crack that my friend had and then I wanted more. Next thing I knew I was at my house getting twenty bucks. I blew off Steve when he asked me what was going on. He had no idea that this was a drug run instead of a beer run. I made two other trips home for more money that night. When I finally got home and went to bed later that night, I was terrified of being addicted. I had heard many stories about crack and how fast it could take a person down. I made a decision right then and there that this would be the last time I would smoke that shit. I did not want to end up acrack-head or worse take one hit and collapse of a brain aneurysm or heart attack. No sir, I would not let that happen.

But as I got ready for work the next day, all I could think about was last night. I thought about it as I walked to the bus stop. I even thought I could smell it as I sat on the bus. I zoned out a few times, feeling glimpses of the high. All day at work I thought about it. As soon as my friend and I got off work that afternoon, we started in on the pipe again. We got into my friend's car to go score a hit. We got the crack and smoked it in the neighborhood park. When we got back into the car and continued driving, suddenly my friend's husband slammed on the brakes and started laughing hysterically. We were only three feet from the Detroit River! I was terrified but in a crazed way, so I started laughing too.

I made another promise to not do any more crack. That promise lasted a week. Then one day at work I learned that the State was going to start random drug testing. I was so afraid of getting caught. I had to stop this madness. I could not lose this good State job. What would my mama think about her baby being a crack head? I decided that I didn't need to smoke crack. I figured that drinking always got me where I need to go. Crack was too dangerous. I weighed the pros and cons and made a very rational decision. It had only been about ten days off and on that I'd smoked it. I stopped going over to my friend's house after work. I knew I was going through withdrawals because, no matter what I was doing, I could taste and smell it. Crack was constantly on my mind. I was very irritable and I could not concentrate. I would sweat though it was not hot. That lasted for about two weeks. Later, I remember being very cocky about it, believing I had such a strong willpower that I was able to quit smoking crack. I would tell myself, feeling powerful, that I had done that on my own.

I began to think that with my strong willpower, I would never get on the wrong side of drinking either. Sure, my father was an alcoholic.

But I believed that I did not have to follow that same path. I didn't know anybody who had such control over crack. Many people got strung out with their first hit. Not me, though. It proved that with my resolve I could also stop drinking whenever I got ready. I felt confident that I could now drink until I had had enough. And I could quit drinking, too, when I was ready.

There were many signs that my drinking was totally out of control. It was getting harder and harder for me to only have a few beers; I would end up drinking anything and everything until it ran out or I passed out. I always woke up with the thought of the next drink. But in my mind this seemed normal and not at all like a dope fiend who needed to steal or do other crimes for their drugs. I acted out in other ways. I spent money that I didn't have. I took money from the bills, or from the food money. I borrowed from family and friends. It became hard to remember who I owed and how much. I had a yellow sticky system at work, because there were folks that I owed there also.

Yet I was not alcoholic; I was just a moderate drinker. When we moved to the house on Park Grove after the fire, it did not take long for me to find the "drinkers" at my new office. Drinkers have a radar for other drinkers. These fellow drinkers protected me by telling me how drink and work could coexist. They told me that when I came to work too hung over to function, to go lie down in the back lounge area until noon. Then we would go out to lunch at the bar across the street, drink a beer to straighten up, and then work the rest of the day. This worked for me for a while. They would cover for me when my hands or voice shook. They'd send me to the back to do some filing so that I wasn't as visible to my supervisor or have to work with the public. The other veteran drinkers would tell me what they did to reduce the shakes and hangover. Don't drink whiskey, or mix the drink with pop, or don't mix it at all. Drink only clear liquor like gin and vodka. Stay away from wine mixed with beer. They did not understand, and neither did I, that I would drink whatever was offered. I had no reservations about the kind of alcohol that I would drink. There was no picking this one brand or type. I didn't discriminate. If it had alcohol in it, I would drink it.

I was getting into trouble at home, too. Although it should have been, home was not a place to escape from work. Home became the place to escape from. My marriage had deteriorated. Steve and I were off doing our own things. He was hustling a lot, working sometimes, and drinking the rest of the time. I was not going to work regularly and I was drinking like a fish. I would disappear for days at a time. My children were beginning to see me do things that no kids should ever see. They had a big aversion to going to school. so most of the time I would just give up trying to get them out of bed. It felt like life was a prison. I drank as often as I could to escape. I would turn up the volume on my stereo. I would go all night until I passed out. I decided that I could not trust myself to go out and drink anymore, so I stopped running off. My life was unraveling fast.

I decided that maybe it would be a good time to put my strong willpower into action. I was ready to stop drinking. I told everybody. I felt that the more people who knew, the more support I would have. Steve, unlike the year before, was glad that I was going to quit. The year before was when he told me that I was not an alcoholic. He told me that I drink just like he did. We would get drunk at home, fight, fallout, wake-up, make love, and start all over again. But those days were gone. I started drinking and never knew what would happen or where I would end up. So my decision to stop drinking worked for a few days. Then one morning I was getting ready for work. Nothing happened to make me think that this day would be different. It was an ordinary day. I came home and cooked dinner. I remember being a bit irritated that I had to cook after being at work all day. With three kids and a husband at home, I would think that somebody would've cooked. Steve was drinking beer so I grabbed one out of refrigerator. A half a pint of Bacardi later, I could not believe I was drunk again. Each time that I set out to quit, I ended up drunk. Then I would be on the floor crying, trying to figure it out. I became suicidal.

One time I remember being so drunk that I could not see the phone. I was crying with snot running down my face. I called 911 and they sent an ambulance for me. This was not the first time these guys had come. They had been in my house before. I had become afraid of overdosing on alcohol, so I would call the paramedics. They would take me to St.

John's Hospital. They would pump me full of fluids to dilute the alcohol in my body. I had done this at least four times. Sometimes it led me to a treatment center. I must've been in every treatment center in the greater Detroit area and even some of the suburbs. But this time was different. The medic brought me into the emergency room where they rolled me into the hallway and left me by a wall because there were no available rooms at that time. I was lying on a gurney in a gown with an IV sticking out of my arm in the middle of the hallway for everybody to see. I saw the medic who brought me in and asked him if he had a spare cigarette. He looked at me with a bit of disgust. As he handed me the cigarette, he looked me dead in my eyes and he said, "You really ought to do something about your drinking, Lady."

In that instant, every bad thing I had ever done in my life was rolled into one big cloud of humiliation. It hovered over me as I took the cigarette. Such shame I felt as I stood there smoking. I had time to digest my life and what the medic had said. I knew he was right. But what I really knew about this scared me: I could not quit drinking. This hit me like a sledgehammer. I was not strong enough. I had no power at all over this. I tried to understand it. Why could I quit crack but I couldn't quit drinking? It made no sense at all. The more I thought about it the more despondent I became. Here I was again at the same place in my life, at another end, another wall. Why was my life so difficult? How are all the other people in the world able to do this life shit? For at least the third time in my life, I did not want to continue living. I was ready to opt out of this life. I was not cut out for this.

Just when I thought I had found my way out of the ghetto, just when I was getting the hang of the world of work, I could have made something of myself. I could've made my mama proud. I was working my way out. But working my way out and alcohol working its way in on me was like a collision that slowly built to an explosion. Work and alcohol. I wanted to work to get out, but alcohol won. I went home. There was nothing more I could do. Even though I knew what the problem was, I had no idea how to fix it. I had no plan B for this. Plan A had been to quit drinking; that didn't happen. Alcohol was stronger than I was.

I tried to go back to work after that paramedic's searing statement. But soon I was back to the bottle. Unable to stay sober long enough to wash up and go to work, soon I was unable to even get out of bed. Steve helped by making sure I had enough to drink. At that point, I was not drinking because I liked it, I was drinking because I had to. Every fiber of my body was telling me that I must drink. I was stuck in between drinking liquor and throwing up bile. There was no reason to eat because it would not stay down. Crackers or toast was my diet. The kids were on autopilot. They would check on me after waking up, and continue on with their day. I found a new way to opt out: if alcohol wanted me, it could have me. I had no more fight left. *Take me quickly, please.* But somewhere in the back of my mind I knew that it wouldn't be a quick deal, that I might have to continue on like that for months. For the next several weeks everything was a blur of sadness-bordering-on-madness with drinking in between. I vaguely remember calling a suicide hotline and being put on hold. My final cry for help and they put me on hold. With my back literally up against the wall, I slid down to the floor. Sobbing so loud I felt it in my soul, I cried out: "God please help me. I can't do this!"

The next day I received a special delivery mail from my job. It looked important. I could not remember how long it had been since I had gone to work. I had stopped calling in with lies about a week before. No need to keep calling in. I could not go back. I had given up. I was going to just die there at home in the hands of the bottle. I could not *not* drink. Shaking, my hands opened up the letter. It said that I was AWOL from work and that this was a final notice for me to come into work or to call. I scoffed to myself: AWOL? I couldn't be AWOL; I was not in the Army. I actually thought that it was quite funny. The State of Michigan cannot make me come to work. I can quit work and I can quit life. I, with my new constant need for alcohol, quit both.

CLIMBING OUT OF THE BARREL

L ater that afternoon there was a knock at the front door. I looked out and there was Dorethea, my coworker. I thought about how we met. I was just getting the hang of things on Gratiot when I got transferred to an office off of the Grand Boulevard. This was, I believe, in response to my drinking and not being dependable. It was hard to get fired from the State of Michigan. They transferred people instead, rotating the problem employees among the different offices.

My new supervisor was a woman named Daisy. She was about five feet tall, and we called her the Tasmanian devil behind her back. I got transferred into that office around the same time that Dorethea got hired. We hit it off very well. Dorethea was a sweet woman with a very nice attitude. She was large and she was gorgeous. She had a little girl and didn't live far from me. Dorethea and I would talk at length about a lot of stuff. She would commiserate with me about Steve and my kids, and I would listen to her talk about how smart her daughter was. I did not know very much about the child's father, only that he did not live with them at the time.

The office on Grand Boulevard took me away from my drinking buddies, who would protect me when I came in smashed or hung over. At this new site I worked with a bunch of straight arrows, folks who went to church and who did not drink like me. They were dependable people. I immediately stuck out like a sore thumb. I went to an office where people did not come in hung over and who worked the full five-day workweek; I was down to about three days that I could manage to get into the office. I did not have any more willpower to not drink just because I was in an office of teetotalers. I'm sure there were some drinkers there but they stayed away from me. I was like a dead man walking and I didn't even know it. I did know that I was being watched. Still, I could not control my actions. When I was there, I worked like three people, if I was not too hung over. Put me to a task and I would get it done and wait for the next one. Dorethea would come in and her only duty was to answer the phone. We were both the backup help for the front reception desk when they were overwhelmed with registrations. They would switch the telephones to us and we would take blue slips and record messages. By now, I was an old hand at this and Dorethea took to it very well also.

There would be times between calls when we would be talking and our supervisor, Daisy, would suddenly appear. She always just sidled up to people very quietly, and she would make a smart-aleck comment like, "You can't talk and work at the same time." She was on me about my work and drinking, and I was the employee she watched like a hawk.

I let Dorethea in. The house was quiet because even though I had stopped living my family continued to live. I don't think they knew the gravity of the decision that I had made. I had come to that place that was the end. I had reached that spot where I had no more hope left. No need in fooling myself, I had lost this fight. I had accepted the fact that I would die a drunk, so I might as well do it at home. There was no more fight left in me. There was no God, no man, no woman who could help. I had given up. So with my coworker standing in my doorway, I figured she had probably come to tell me that I had been fired. So what? I was done anyway. I was kind of relieved to see her though. We sat down. She asked me why I had stopped coming to work.

My mind went straight to formulating a lie. Lying was quite automatic. I wondered which lie I should tell. I didn't feel well? No. For some reason, I told her the truth. "I can't do this anymore." I explained how I just couldn't work. That I was tired of trying to work. That I had so many problems. That I couldn't stop drinking.

With the love of a true friend, she looked me in my eyes and I could see that she loved me. She said, "Brenda, everyone has problems. But everyone doesn't drink to solve their problems." These words were the same ones I had heard before from other people. But for some reason, the meaning of these words became suddenly clear. I admitted to myself, that I couldn't be the only person in the world with the types of problems I had. Dorethea went on to tell me that if I came back to work I could get help for my problems. What was most important to me was when she said that she would help. Dorethea would be there to help me through this.

So, suddenly I was not drinking but I was miserable. I would watch Steve and our friends drinking and wonder why they got to enjoy themselves. Even worse, Steve usually used my money to buy the beer, wine, and liquor. That really made me angry. I had no release for what I felt. I felt angry at the world and everyone in it. One day Steve went to the liquor store for more booze and he came back with six-pack of near beer (2% alcohol but labeled as non-alcoholic). Steve was only trying to help. He saw how miserable I was when I was not drinking. I had been alcohol-free for about a week. I was a complete mess. My family never knew who I was going to be; one minute I was nice and the next I was angry, distraught, crying, or mean. Steve told me that this near beer would not get me drunk or into trouble because it didn't contain enough alcohol. It didn't take much for me to believe this. My body was craving alcohol. I wanted to drink like everyone else. It was very easy to believe that the near beer would allow me to drink like my friends.

Steve wanted the old me back and so did my kids. Better the devil they knew than the unpredictable mess I had become. I did not realize that removing the alcohol and not replacing it with something else was the problem. I had not yet grasped any of the concepts around the addiction that I had. I did not know about my body dynamics and how my body craved alcohol. I had become an alcoholic, but all I knew was that I was not happy when I did not drink. Not being happy was an understatement. I could not get my mind to stop thinking about alcohol. This was worse than the cravings that I had for crack. I felt like every fiber in my body was pulsating with the thought of drinking. I felt hot and cold at the same time. I was sad, depressed, ashamed, and felt like a failure because I was an alcoholic. I just did not understand. How did people do it?

How could I do it? Before I took a sip of the near beer, I had hundred of these thoughts go through my mind. Thoughts of how I would be successful this time. Maybe it was all a mistake and I was not an alcoholic. Nowhere in all of these thoughts were there any recollections of the pain and heartache of my last drinking episode.

The bottle of near beer felt cold and good in my hand. I opened it. I could see the bubbles rising up to the top. I put the bottle to my mouth and took a small sip as if I was being tentative. I did not want Steve to see how desperate I really was for alcohol. The near beer was nasty tasting. I took another sip. Then I began to feel my body and my mind shift into a different gear. I took a deeper swallow and that was it; I was drinking again. Drinking normally. I took a deep sigh. My blood began to flow and my mind became alert. Almost at once, I became a better person. I was almost happy. I felt like I could be myself again, the old Brenda. Steve and I sat there drinking. He was drinking regular beer and I was drinking near beer. This continued all week long. I could not wait to show off my ability to control my drinking. When we would go across the street to visit friends, or if we went over to my sister's house, I would take a six-pack of near beer to show everyone that I had this thing under control. I could drink like others without getting into trouble.

That next week it all changed.

Everyday I could not wait to get home so I could drink my near beer. I would rush home, go to the corner store, and buy my six-pack. The second week of drinking smarter seem to make me smarter too. It dawned on me how well I was doing. Maybe I was not an alcoholic after all. Maybe I was blowing this thing way out of proportion. I did not think of any of the times that I drank before and had problems. I walked into the liquor store and glanced at the small airplane-size bottles of Bacardi rum behind the bulletproof plexiglas. I walked past them to the back of the store to the beer in the coolers, but the rum had registered in my mind. As I looked at the near beer, I saw that the price was $ 2.29 for a six-pack. I thought about how I could get liquor for the same price and I would not have to keep running back and forth to the store. A half pint of Bacardi rum would be about the same price. I thought I was very smart to figure that out. I could save money, save myself a trip to the store, get half a bottle of rum, and be done with it. I put the near beer back in the cooler, walked up to the counter and told the store clerk to give me a half pint of Bacardi Rum. Walking home, I felt so smug. At no time did memories of the previous screw-ups enter my mind: my drunk episodes, overdoses, passing out at home and at work, cussing, fights, falling on my head, or missing work. I could have the rum because I had no problem drinking near beer for a week and a half.

Lord, I didn't want to suffer anymore! I had tried psychiatric help, emergency rooms, hospitals and IVs, crack and near beer. I was tired and desperate. The near beer had taken me right back to drinking until I could not drink anymore. So I got up the courage. Shaking, I sat on the edge of my bed. I called the information line and asked for help. I got a number for a different office. It took me another hour to dial the second number because I needed to think about it a little bit more. Once I did call, I told the guy who answered that I wanted help for my drinking. He suggested a place I could go that was within walking distance from my home.

I remember the look on Tamiko's face as she watched me write down the address. She was the oldest and had seen the most. She looked like she was afraid to have hope, afraid of being led to the top of a building and dropped off the edge once again. I told her what the guy said. She and Michaell were looking at me trying to figure it all out. Should they even get their hopes up? Tamiko said, "We can walk you there, Mama, so you don't have to go alone." I could not let her see the fear in me. I also could not let her down this time. She believed that this might help and I could see that in her eyes. I got up off my bed and put on jeans and a sweater that I pulled from the top of a pile of dirty clothes on the floor. I grabbed a knit skullcap for my head because I had not done anything to my hair. I stood there afraid to move. Tamiko and Michaell were waiting for me by the front door and out into the cold we went. I held both of my girls' hands as we walked. Tamiko asked me questions that I could not answer.

When we found the building, I swallowed my fear and took my first step through the door. I pulled my skullcap down over my eyes and looked around. It was a weird place. I had made a vow to myself to stay in the background, to try not to stand out. But when I was asked, I found myself raising my hand to indicate that I was new. It was astonishing to me, as if someone else was in control of my hand. Despite the cold outside, I felt hot and sweaty. The next thing I knew, the guy who seemed to be in charge was welcoming me. He reassured me that if I had a problem with alcohol I could find help there. Immediately, I thought those people were hokey. They talked, read stuff aloud, and introduced themselves to me. It seemed like there were some rules printed up on the wall. At some point, someone said something about God and I wondered how I might feel about that, not sure that I was interested in a religious thing. These folks were not very much like me, I decided, because they seemed to believe that their drinking was a problem over which they had no control. They talked about how they might be able to beat their alcoholism by doing a few things.

Right off the bat I said to myself, "Okay, I can do those things, too." The people at the gathering gave me some stuff to take with me to read. Back at home, I thought about everything. I decided that with my college degree, I was well equipped to do the homework assignment I'd been given. I had no intention of going back there though. I'd had harder homework projects. I could easily do it on my own.

The next thing I knew, the heavy doom fell over me again. I was afraid and hopeless. How. Did. I. Get. Here. Again? It was as if I never stopped drinking. I felt like I was back on a hamster wheel, only this time I had no fight left. I picked up my bottle and finished my rum. Might as well. The alcohol had me beat. I was done. I totally gave up. There was a sense of peace in this; I felt resigned with my failure. Alcohol gave me the thing that no one else was able to. It allowed me to be at ease. It made me feel safe. I could just be. It had worked for years; then it didn't. It was who I was. There was no changing.

My life was one endless ball of turmoil. I was tired of waiting for my life to get better. I was tired of waiting for my kids to grow up so I could leave Steve. I was tired of not getting any relief from alcohol. I was tired in my soul and in my heart. Drinking even stopped taking the tired away. It was more like a crazy numbness. I longed for what I used to have. Drinking used to make me feel joy, but there was no more joy. Instead, I had only fear, regret, and guilt. What had I done what my life? I was thirty-four years old with three children that I was finding hard to care for and protect, and a husband who I felt was not man enough to take responsibility for his family. The problem I thought was with Steve. He kept drinking and so did everyone I knew. I would tell them I was not drinking, that I was trying to quit. There was no one in my life who understood. It was as if I was being set up to fail.

RECOVERY, IN OUT IN

I believe we get grace in this life. I know I've received my share of it. In my depression I often wondered why God had left me, never thinking that He would already be there when I was ready. As I sat at home one day, some of the things I'd heard that night with the recovering drinkers started gaining volume in the back of my head. They had encouraged me to come back to their gatherings. Then I got a thought as clear as if someone was right there speaking it to me. *Why don't I go back to see them?* I felt totally ashamed that I was drinking again. But then I was given a sliver of grace: if they were drunks like me, surely they would know that I have problems with my drinking. I remembered that they met every day at 6:00. I got myself together and went over there. I had lost all of the smugness of before. I walked in broken, with my head down and my tail between my legs.

A coworker I had seen the other time I was there, and who had reassured me they'd all be there waiting for me when I was ready, was standing just inside the door. He said, "Welcome home." I was shocked. How did he know I suddenly felt these people were like me? We all were misfits in the same family with the same master cracking the whip and beating us into submission. Yet, my coworker and a lot of the others seemed to look a little less whipped than I felt. Whatever they were doing looked like it was working, though it was a mystery to me. Sometimes they laughed, which I couldn't understand in all my pain that night. But I listened to their stories and even found the courage to say something about myself. I realized that they really knew exactly how I was feeling. They could laugh with me, and say, "Yes, I did that also when I was drinking."

But what was clear was how I felt after that first time back: I knew I was not alone. I thought that this could actually work for me. There were people there who talked about drinking and doing some of the same things I had done. But they were getting better. I felt hope inside for the first time in ages. The sharing of stories had a profound effect on me. This was a group of people willing to tell me what happened to them, so that I could see that they were like me. To be able to identify with these people would be the first step along a sober path. I began to get together with them regularly, even daily. The things that they read each time we got together increased my hope. Eventually I was staying sober day by day just by hanging out with them and fighting the urge to drink.

I got into new routines and habits. Before I had a car, people I vaguely knew would offer to take me to the gathering places where these non-drinking alcoholics would hang out. Every day I still wanted to drink. Even though I craved alcohol, something was working because I had not caved in to the craving. My work habits improved. I poured all of my energy into going to work and working on my recovery. With every day that I did not drink, I began to get a sense of accomplishment. But I was also scared.

I learned that we shared some of the same problems. We were all miserable from drinking, and we all saw how drinking had wrecked our lives. These people started out as strangers but even when I was new, they all reached out to me. I could tell that they cared about me. They wanted to give me suggestions for how they had stopped drinking, and most of all, for how they coped with daily life. I began to care about these people, in return. I met a woman who became my mentor in life, to help me through recovery. This former prostitute, drug user, and alcoholic would become one of my closest friends. She was funny and down to earth.

This mentor taught me how to be a woman and a mother. I confided my entire life story to her and she helped me see that being an alcoholic was not my own or anyone else's fault. She told me that all I had to do was to believe that she believed that God would help me. She was one of the many women that I met and learned to rely on as I walked my way out of the darkness of alcohol addiction.

Yes, alcohol still called to me. Steve was drinking, as were my family and friends. But I accepted the fact that I could not drink. Taking even one sip was like starting a chain of events that always led to the same dark oblivion. So I began to think, believe, and behave as my new community of people did.

People who knew me noticed the change in me before I did. My family and work friends frequently told me that I looked better. I thought it was because I was taking better care of myself: not dressing while drunk, washing myself, doing laundry. But they described it as a calm, a peace, they saw. What I felt inside was more of an acceptance. I accepted that I had a problem that I could not solve. I acknowledged that God could help me solve it. I did still believe in God; though at first I felt unworthy to receive His help, given all that I had done while I was drinking.

My job was changing. It was as if I got what I needed but had not even figured out that I needed it. I was put in charge of the office supply inventory. My new workstation was a closet sized office. I was embarrassed for my coworkers to see me reading about recovery, so I would keep the door closed. When I first got moved to the supply office, I was angry. I felt that it was a punishment. Eventually, I accepted it and started realizing that I could use the time alone in the closet to read and to think about my life. Day by day, I began to just listen and do what I saw the other people doing. Being sober was hard.

But I also experienced miracles large and small as I continued on the path of recovery. One chilly, windy October day I was walking to meet my friends. I was dressed in many layers under my lightweight jacket. I was cold. I was thinking about my check from work and how I just might have a little money left over after bills. I was somewhat at a crossroads because the gas had been shut off for the past two weeks and it was cold enough in the house to notice one's breath. So I was walking and thinking about which problem to solve, gas or coat. I remember walking and saying an informal prayer for God to help me know. When I got home the kids told me that a woman from the community of recovering alcoholics had stopped by and dropped off a nice warm coat. She had seen me and thought that I could use it. Little miracle number one!

It was from the others that I learned some basics about how to live day to day. I learned about financial responsibility. Though working, I always felt stuck in a hole and didn't know how to get out. Even after I got sober, I continued to cash my paychecks at the corner liquor store, which cost a fortune. A friend in recovery told me about getting a bank account at the local credit union, a perk of my job. My paychecks were then deposited electronically, saving me the cashing fee. Shady deals on house refinancing and filing bankruptcy—ideas that Steve had—negatively impacted my credit. After I learned that Steve was siphoning money out of our joint account, another sober friend told me how to have a separate account just for paying bills.

At this point, my family knew that this was sticking. I became aware of things that I could not see while I was drinking. My kids had grown up. Tamiko and Michaell had grown into teenagers. Aaron was becoming a little man. They were proud of me for working on my recovery. But they also did not want to get their hopes dashed again if I fell off the wagon. I was not the Screaming Mimi my kids had gotten used to. There were many disagreements with my girls during that time, but I handled them with a calm and rationality that was supplemented by input from my vast community of wise mentors. Tamiko and Michaell had the hardest time dealing with this new mama. There were fights. Tamiko would move out sometimes taking Michaell with her. I learned to just let them go. Steve accused me of being too calm about it, too detached. What he did not realize was that when I had an issue, whether it was at home or work, my new behavior was to not jump into action but to pause and try to understand the issue, maybe seeking counsel from someone who had gone through the same thing. A wise one pointed out to me that I didn't need to be right to be happy. I just needed to come to a common ground with my kids. I didn't have to be a dictator, ruling with an iron fist.

I had already taught my kids right from wrong. I needed to give them space. No matter how hard I wanted to shield them from pain, they needed that pain so they could learn life lessons. I was learning how to be a mother. I had only a few tools for this. My mother did not live long enough to show me. There was no instruction manual. All I knew is that I loved them with everything in me. I was a mama bear protecting my cubs.

My marriage was basically over. Steve could not or would not forgive all of my transgressions from my drinking days. I had left home for two or three days at a stretch. I had affairs with other men. I said horrible things to him when I was drunk. I could forgive him, but I could never forget the fights and all of the times he had hit me, or that time he came home with panties in the glove box of his car. I couldn't forget the time he threw me down the stairs, fracturing my arm. I could see that Steve was holding me back. I would pray for my kids and for Steve. I prayed for safety. I prayed for God to get me out of the neighborhood we were living in; a murder next door to my house and having our home broken into many times were now part of the neighborhood. So I went to work and I went to recovery gatherings, all the while praying for the strength to continue.

I felt like every decision happening in my life was a direct result of my faith in God. I finally figured out that what He wanted for me was a better life. We were partners in this thing: my life. All I had to do was to follow the plan. There were directions laid out in front of me. Allowing myself to believe that inner voice meant that I had to ignore the other voice that always took precedence in my head.

The hateful voice inside was always ready to tell me that I was black, baldheaded and ugly, stupid, dumb and a bad mother, a slut who would never amount to anything. That was the voice that alcohol and drugs fed. I thought alcohol and drugs quieted these down and they did for a while, until they wanted more; then the voices returned and drowned out any faith in myself or in God. But now I knew what peace felt like. I was not going to give that up for anything in the world.

I entered this pact with my higher power. I would continue to follow direction and He would continue to take care of me. I knew after this that I would be okay. For the first time in my life, I felt in my soul that I was being taken care of. I felt grace at last. There was peace in my heart but there was still hell in my home. Faith gave me greater ambition.

I had been told since I was a little girl that I acted like I thought I was better than everyone else. Maybe it was something deep within, my desire to reach for more than I had. I always felt that there was more to this life. Even when I was at my lowest, I felt that there should be more in my life. As I got sober, I learned that I could live like normal people, that I could have a good life. I began to remember more of my mama's wisdom. She had told me how to "get out." I had just been diverted off of the path for a while.

I began to dream of a better life at home and at work. I heard an analogy about how my life was like being in a barrel of crabs. When fishermen catch crabs, they are all put into one barrel. They attempt to get out by climbing on the backs of the other crabs. When one manages to get to the top of the heap, just as it seems close to escaping, the rest of the crabs grab him and pull him back down into the barrel. That one crab can't get free because all of the other crabs keep pulling him back in again. This is the way I felt about everyone in my immediate circle. I was starting to see a bit clearer without the alcohol. I could see what and who was holding me back, who the crabs were.

JOB TRAINING, OVERACHIEVER

I thought that it was time for me to move out of the inventory closet where I'd spent the bulk of my workday since returning to my job and getting into recovery. I began to believe that I could not just survive at work but that I could get promoted like I saw my other clerical friends doing. Small changes in my confidence began to develop. I got two job promotions during that first year and a half of sobriety. This took me to the top of the pay scale for clerical workers. I was making around $12.00 an hour.

That first year back was such hard work but it was worth it as I began to dream bigger dreams. I began to believe that I could go as far as God wanted me to go. From my friends in recovery, I heard that getting sober was one piece of the pie. But if I were to take advantage of this gift of sobriety, I should shoot for the whole pie rather than a mere slice. I decided to do just that. I wanted it all: vacations, a husband who loved me, to have fun, to not be afraid all the time. Fear was what had driven most of my decisions before recovery. This new way of living would help to reduce my fears, I was told. Now that I was out of the inventory closet, I was showing the supervisors and district managers that I was reliable and that they had made the right decision in giving me a second chance.

At this time in my life, Steve and I were still struggling at home. Even with my new salary it was hard. I no longer had the welfare net to fall back on. My light, gas, and water bills were astronomical. There were times when payment in full was necessary in order to keep the service on, but I never had enough money to do so. I had been paying on my bills all of my life. I learned that from welfare. They only gave me a fixed amount of money each month and that's what I was used to paying. The same services that could help poor people pay shut-off notices were no longer available to help me once my income increased.

The next obvious step up was to become a social worker. I had all of the qualifications. Social work was hard and most workers had large caseloads. They complained every day. But I looked at it as another piece of the pie. My first transfer and promotion was to Warren, Michigan where I worked as an entry-level social worker. I was now truly interacting with people in need.

I remember thinking, "Wow! I'm on the other side of the desk now." Working in Warren was very different. The clients tended to be more middle-class. I was sent for a two-month training at the main office downtown. We were required to learn all of the basic policies and standards, which, at times, felt like standing in front of a fire hose. It did, though, give me time to reflect back on my reliance on welfare. I got to understand the history of the services and how welfare had been a direct result of helping people after the Depression. Although the services were meant to be temporary, some people found themselves trapped in the system.

Like my family, it became generational. So I began to believe that maybe I could break that pattern. My children did not have to follow in my footsteps, living a life on welfare. I could pass down to them the ethics of work instead of how to make food stamps stretch. I also could show them, by example, that this was the life we were meant to live. I began to preach to them about how God has a plan for all of us and how we were not meant to suffer in this life. Even though they rolled their eyes when I got on one of these rants, I could tell that they wanted to believe it.

Warren had a 90% white population. So it didn't take long for me to encounter people who, on both sides of the desk, had an opinion on the color of my skin. There were rumors about managers who called the three of us black employees "monkeys" behind our backs, or clients who thought that it was okay to express their opinions on that matter. Most of the remarks that I heard from clients revolved around a misperception that they had been denied full benefits because they were white. The truth is that they had assets which the system expected them to sell before they would be considered eligible for support.

The system was especially hard on the elderly who also had social security benefits but still couldn't make ends meet. I found myself pulling out these huge policy books trying to help folks, only to be shown by my supervisor why we could not help. The people who most needed help were not getting it. But there were others who knew how to work the system. It was disheartening to not be able to help those who really needed it but to see how others manipulated the process to receive full benefits. There I was after all I had been through, trying to find fairness in life. I began to care about my clients. I developed a protective attitude about some of the people on my caseload. I would call them to remind them to get their monthly paperwork in on time so that they would not lose benefits. My caseload was huge and I was overwhelmed. I started to feel that all I was doing was applying a Band-Aid to a chest wound. People needed help and I was making them jump through hoops to get it. I felt bad about that.

After a year I decided that I was not cut out to be a social worker. I felt that the system was broken, and had been for a long time. I went back to clerical work. I just needed more peace of mind. Working back in clerical felt good at first. I could do the things that I was good at: filing, answering phones, and organizing. Here I could see progress. I could take a stack of documents and have them filed in an hour. That was what I needed. I could not see progress in the casework.

Then, I was asked to substitute for the Children's Protective Services clerical worker for three days. Working for CPS, I began to get a different insight into the thoughts and behaviors of parents who were, for many reasons, unable to cope with the job of raising children. One of my main tasks was to type up the verbal case recordings that workers made after every home visit. Listening to the things that adults did to children weighed on my soul; little, innocent babies and children were being abused by the very people who were responsible for taking care of them.

Then there were those parents who, even though they were incapable of taking care of the kids, would go to any lengths to keep them. It was 1998 and I was working in Macomb County when Lisa's Law got enacted. Lisa Putman was a CPS worker who had been caught between a mother and the children they both wanted to protect. Lisa was making a routine home visit alone when the mother dragged her into the house and beat her to death with a baseball bat. The mother mistakenly thought that Lisa was there to remove the children from the home for neglect. After this happened, our whole office had to have grief counseling. This set the stage for many changes in the way social workers were trained and protected. I had only talked to Lisa a few times but it had a significant impact on me. After my short stint as a social worker, I realized I wanted to continue working my way up the ladder. Social work was just a steppingstone along my career path.

Around that same time, I was taking classes on and off. One night after work, a woman who had been in recovery longer than me shared about how she was almost finished with her nursing degree. She talked about the freedom and sense of accomplishment she felt. I looked at her in awe. She was at the end of a four-year endeavor. I could do that! Why not go back to what I loved? I felt upbeat and carried a new resolve. I promised myself that I'd begin investigating what it would take to finally finish my Bachelor's degree. Within the next few days I had the information I needed and I planned out my next year of required courses.

The State of Michigan was making the leap into the computer age. Our office had a computer room in which thirty employees shared six computers and ran client budgets on antiquated systems. The state pulled information from their employee files to look for any employees who might have earned an associate or bachelor degree in computer science. My name popped up for Macomb County. I was elated when my supervisor told me that they would send me to a six-month intensive training program to learn how to be the expert in computers for Macomb County. This is exactly what I wanted to get my foot in the door, to walk out of clerical and social work into the bright lights of computer and technology.

Though the personal computer was a relatively new concept, I had rented one from a rent-to-own store and taught myself how to use email and the Internet; this allowed me to stay just ahead of the curve. During the training, I did not work in my Warren office. We learned all of the latest technologies and programs, as well as about input and output devices, troubleshooting, and future trends. This whole industry was moving at the speed of light. We were a class of sixteen of Michigan's brightest. We spent over three hundred hours on training, after which we were presented with a certificate of completion from the Lansing Computer Institute. My new title at work became: Brenda Fantroy, Information System Support Technician. Almost everything had fallen into place at work. My job was exciting. A whole new world of technology had opened up for me. My self-esteem was slowly being repaired. I was recovering some peace. I worked in this new job, commuting back and forth every day.

My boss was one of the first black district managers of Macomb County. She had taught me a lot about how to deal with being black in a mostly white environment, including how to remain professional even when pushed. Her office became a safe place for me to blow off steam. She helped usher in respect for the black employees by outlining an office policy that spelled out exactly what was expected of us. This helped to identify our duties to the rest of the office so that we were elevated from office staff to technology professionals. In time, the culture of the workplace changed and we were given respect and valued for more than changing the printer paper. My relationship with my boss had been very good. I thought of her as a mentor. I would listen to her talk about her children and knew that she had grown up in the suburbs of a nice, mostly-white area of town.

One day after receiving a very favorable employee evaluation, I asked my boss for raise. She told me that I would get the typical 2% increase, but that she could not give me more. I asked why, and she indicated that it would be too much trouble for her to make the request. My boss went on to say that if I really needed extra money, maybe I should get a second job. It was in that moment that our relationship changed. I recalled all that she had taught me about professionalism and poise. I thanked her for her evaluation and calmly walked out of the office. I sat at my desk and then went outside for a walk. My head felt like it was on fire. I needed to vent but felt there was no one and nowhere in the office to do that. As I walked I just kept thinking, "How dare she suggest I get a second job!" I knew how much she made because salary information for state employees was public knowledge. It was nearly double what I made. I raged within myself. Then, a calm came over me. I suddenly realized that in order to earn more, I had to move on to a place where the pay scale was better; I had reached my limit in that office. From that point on, I became really competitive at work. I knew that I had the brains to move up. I just needed to be dedicated. I needed to have a strategy. I began to not only dress for success, I also acted as if I was already successful. I applied for technical positions in Lansing, Michigan because the heart of the state's computer networks was located there.

It was the perfect time to make a change. I felt more confident in myself. My recovery was going well. I had started to believe that I could have a happy life. I just needed to do a few things first. I needed to divorce my husband. We were never going to be happy. We had too much deceit and violence between us to forgive each other. I needed to move with my kids out of the madness of Detroit. If I wanted a new start, it would have to be in a place where I did not know where all the bodies were buried. My plan was to leave Steve and Detroit behind, to take my three children and start a new life in Lansing. I needed to finally be free of the crime and drugs that had taken over the city. I was driven by this new plan. It gave me hope and it fulfilled my dreams on so many levels. I had not had this much hope for my life in a long time. I felt as if my window on the world had just opened wide enough to see. Maybe I would be able to get out. But I had to be careful, and to execute each piece of the plan with diligence.

I finally got the job interview in Lansing at the State's Grand Tower Building. I remember how nervous and afraid I was. The week before the interview I did a drive-by. This was before the use of the GPS. Following the route on paper maps, I drove the hundred and eighty round-trip miles, ninety minutes each way, just so I would know where I was going. I knew I was qualified for this job so I did a lot of research on how to interview, what questions to ask, what they would ask me. I practiced by looking at myself in the mirror. I smiled and listened intently. I even went to the Goodwill and bought a new dress suit. I was prepared.

I walked into the huge building the next day. This Grand Tower world was brand new to me. The building was nine stories high and sat in the heart of downtown, four blocks from the state capital and alongside the Grand River. The only river I had seen in my entire life prior to then was the Detroit River.

When I got there, I presented myself to the guard at the front desk telling him that I had an appointment. He looked through his book and told me that my appointment was for tomorrow; my heart sank. In all of my excitement, I had shown up a day early! Wow, I felt stupid. Maybe I was not ready for the big time. Maybe I should just run back to Detroit and give up this crazy idea. Maybe I was asking for too much. I walked out of the Grand Tower and back to my car. There was a bench in the back of the building facing the river. I thought it would be a good idea to sit and collect myself here before I drove back. I sat and watched the water flow. The water was brown and it was swift. I began to think about all of the life that must be living under the surface. I thought about how small I felt in the great scheme of things. How the fish did not know I even existed. Then all of a sudden I felt a peace, a calm, come over me. And in that instant I knew that I was on the right path. I knew in every fiber of my being that I was just where I should be. It was the chance that I needed. It felt almost like euphoria: light, but all consuming. It draped over me like a cloak and in the next moment it was gone. But it was enough. I got in my car and drove home. I drove back the next day and had the interview. I knew I had the job before I walked out the door from my interview.

I began to reap the benefits of the many good habits I had developed over five years of sobriety. I had a habit of telling the truth, partly because I learned that it was much easier than lying. I practiced looking people in the eyes instead of looking down as I spoke. Also, I learned that even though I was afraid, fear could work for me. I combatted fear with faith. I prayed a lot and I was amazed how I could follow through with something despite my fear. I had finished both my associate and bachelor degrees, and was working in my field of study. I had the inner drive to make my mama's dream come true: to get myself and my kids out of the ghetto. There was no stopping me.

After getting hired to work in my field of technology in the Grand Tower in Lansing— the first "best job of my life" —I thought about the younger Brenda riding the bus and looking up at the tall office buildings of GM and Burroughs. I remember thinking that one day I would be sitting on the top floor, working an office job from 8 o'clock to 5 o'clock, going to lunch with my buddies, wearing sharp clothes to work. This was my dream come true.

Faith was increased for me when there was evidence to back it up. I eventually became so calm and assured of my direction that it was like I was being propelled on my journey by my belief alone. I felt like there was not any decision happening in my life that was not a direct result of my faith in God. God and I were on the same page.

HARVEY

he first time I met Harvey was on a retreat; it was an encounter that did not go well. My mentor had invited me to go with her for a weekend on the outskirts of Detroit. This annual event always occurred in December and was open to men and women. I remember talking Steve into letting me go. It took a lot of convincing, and he was still mad that I was going. I told Steve that I didn't think anybody would be sleeping together there, if that was his worry. The retreat was being held at a Catholic monastery.

I was very new in my recovery, so I was still a nervous wreck. I only knew a few of the few dozen folks who would be in attendance. The monastery allowed us to smoke in the basement of the building. So I spent a lot of time down there trying to figure out how to act, and to understand what I should be doing on the retreat. I was sitting drinking coffee and smoking a Newport cigarette when a tall, white man came over to me. He asked how I was doing. Without skipping a beat, I gave my standard answer that I was fine. And then he, a total stranger, said with a smirk on his face, "Well, you ought to let your face know it." I was taken aback and suddenly at a loss for words. I did not like this man and in the two seconds after that exchange, I had devised in my head the many ways I could think of to take his smart ass out.

I walked over to my mentor and asked her who that white guy was, pointing toward him. She told me his name was Harvey. She then told me what she knew about him. Apparently, he was there with his fourth wife. The wife was in some sort of a Ph.D. program and Harvey was a big shot in the recovery circles, having started a club in the ritzy Grosse

Pointe neighborhood. I told my mentor that I did not really care who he was, that he had a smart mouth and I knew some boys back in Detroit who could take care of that for me. Of course, though that was what I told her, the truth was that I didn't personally know anybody. I was just mad that I did not have a snappy comeback for Harvey. During the rest of the retreat, I stayed away from Harvey and his wife.

The second time I encountered Harvey, about six months later, someone introduced us. I remembered him from the retreat. We were at one of the gatherings of people in recovery from alcoholism. It was my turn to tell everyone about how I got into recovery, and what I had been doing to stay sober for the past six years. Harvey was leading the group that night. I practically ignored him, mainly because my dad was there also.

I had mentioned to Daddy that I would be speaking and he caught the bus from the west side of Detroit to see his baby girl speak. I was glad to see my dad even though he showed up drunk. At the end of my talk, Harvey said, "Brenda did not blame anyone for her drinking—not her mom, her dad, or growing up in Detroit."

Right then, Daddy jumped up and shouted, "Yeah, that's my baby"! I was kind of embarrassed, but more proud than not. I felt that maybe I had gotten back a little of my good girl status.

I lost track of Harvey for a few years after that. When our paths crossed again, he showed up at another of the recovery gatherings. I remember him standing in the back of the room with his white-man business uniform on: khaki pants, blue button-down shirt with a V-neck sweater, and brown dress shoes. That time he looked different. I remember thinking about how it seemed the last few years had not been kind to him. He had lost some weight and he looked lost. Of course, I was able to get the backstory from other people who knew Harvey. It turns out that he and his fourth wife had gone through a nasty divorce. Our mutual friends were worried about him living all alone so far away in Massachusetts (where he'd ended up), so they invited Harvey to return to Detroit. Harvey often showed up to our group after that. About that same time, though, I began to commute to Lansing and Harvey became just another guy in the group.

This changed on a particular Saturday when I looked around and noticed that Harvey was not at the group gathering. I nonchalantly asked someone where he was. My buddy smiled, telling me that Harvey was out on a date with a good friend of mine. This good friend was the first person to take me under her wing when I was new in recovery; she drove me around the city to various gatherings of other people who wanted to stop drinking. If she could not take me herself, she always found someone who could. Because this friend lived near me, I had often walked to her house and sat crying on her stoop with some huge problem or another. I would sit and wait for her to come home. Sometimes she did; sometimes she didn't. But her house was always a safe place for me. Even so, when my buddy told me that this good friend and Harvey were out on a date, something that I can't explain came over me. I was instantly jealous, although I did not recognize it at the time. I thought it was anger, and I thought I was hiding my feelings. I even tried to cover up how I was feeling by telling my buddy I hoped Harvey bought her flowers. Everybody knows that's what is supposed to happen when someone is taken out on a date; though that had never happened for me. I never dated. I was never formally asked out. I met men and I never, ever got flowers. Of course, my buddy saw that I was jealous and I could see in his face that he could not wait to tell Harvey about it.

About a week later I saw Harvey again. My normal way of being attracted to guys had changed. Usually all a guy had to do was say hi or act like they were interested and that was all that was needed. My imagination would have us dating and married all within the same day. I had no idea of how to have a real relationship or friendship with a man. When I saw Harvey, I tried to not show that I was interested in him. I could not afford to be at that point in my life. My plan to move out of the city was going well. I really did not need to complicate my life any further. But my higher power had other plans. Harvey came over to me and we started talking. I don't remember what we talked about, but I knew that this was different. This was the beginning of something.

I DON'T BELONG HERE

I felt good when I talked to Harvey. He seemed shy around me at first like he didn't know quite how to talk to me. I had butterflies in my stomach and got all tongue-tied every time I talked to him. When he spoke among our friends in recovery, I was alert and attentive. I was enchanted. This attraction was quick and it was deep.

Eventually he brought up the subject of going out to lunch. I didn't want to seem too interested, but I was. I jokingly told him that I worked miles away in Lansing. I figured those ninety miles would deter most men. It was as if Lansing was a faraway land that people from Detroit, people in my circle, would never travel to especially for lunch. Harvey told me that would not be a problem. So I gave him my work number and he said he would call me.

At the time I thought that he would figure out that Lansing was really too far to travel to take somebody to lunch and he would just back out. What I really felt was that I was not worth it. I had decided that this was over before it started, and I really felt that it might be for the best. I was trying to walk a straight path, not so much to be faithful to Steve, but to live my life different than I was doing before. Flirting was one of the things I thought I needed to stop doing in order to keep my promise to this new way of life. Beware of my beginnings and the end will take care of itself, is what I had heard. I was shocked when Harvey called me at work a few days later saying that he was in the lobby and he would like to take me to lunch. What kind of man does that? Drive over one hundred miles to take someone to lunch? I was worried. Maybe there was something wrong with this guy. I had never really dated anyone, let alone a white guy, so how should I act? Thank God I was wearing one of my nice dress-for-success outfits. I told him that I would be down shortly; I got myself together and got on the elevator. All the while I was wondering what I had gotten myself into. I was sure that everyone I saw could see a scarlet letter on my forehand.

Harvey looked good but there was something else. There was confidence. He looked as though he knew exactly what he wanted. As we walked out of the revolving door and down Grand Avenue, I was aware that everything around me was normal. I was also aware that Harvey and I seemed to be in our own little bubble. He slyly reached for my hand as we were walking. It felt like a jolt of electricity. I pulled my hand back, reminding him that I was married and my coworkers knew that. He smiled, and I noticed that I liked his smile. As we continued down Grand Avenue, I began to wonder where he was taking me because most of the restaurants were located up on First Street. I didn't voice my concern. We didn't talk much. We just kept walking.

We came to the next block and I noticed the only building in this block was the Sheraton Hotel. I panicked. I thought to myself, *oh no, he can't be thinking what I'm thinking.* We continued toward the hotel. I looked up at him in disbelief and said, "I'm not going to a hotel with you! What kind of girl do you think I am?" He opened the heavy door and held it for me, telling me as we walked through the lobby that there was a restaurant in the hotel. He smiled. I almost died of embarrassment.

We were seated. I was very nervous. I learned some things on that first date. I learned that spaghetti does not make a great date food. I learned that I knew nothing about salad forks or dessert spoons. Napkins that are on plates need to go in the lap. I did know to keep my elbows off the table; I remembered my mama teaching me that. I figured my best bet was the old monkey-see, monkey-do deal. So I sat and watched Harvey and picked at my food.

Harvey was a talker and a salesman who traveled a lot. Going up to Lansing from Detroit for lunch was not a big deal for him. He drove all over the state as well as out of state. He talked like a world traveler but it may have just been me being mesmerized by his sales pitch. He launched right into this dialogue about what he was looking for in a woman. Of course, I didn't register it as a pitch so much as him being a bit pushy. He talked about the woman he was looking for. She would have to be able to travel. He wanted someone who liked hiking and camping. He was prepared to go on, but I stopped him right there. "Harvey, this is just a date." I thought to myself about the more pertinent issues we'd have before us if this continued. To begin with, I'm black and he's white; we will have to get over that hurdle first. We finished up the meal and walked back to my office.

I thanked him for lunch and he said he'd call me. I told him not to call me, that I would call him. In the elevator after saying goodbye, I knew what it was that I had to do. I got to my desk and sat there for a few seconds. It was going too fast. I couldn't have a relationship with this man. I'm not prepared; I have too much to do. This is not part of my plan. What was God trying to do to me? What did he mean, putting this man into my life? Maybe this was a test of some sort. I really wanted to see where this relationship would go. I was so attracted to Harvey that it scared me. But, why now? I knew what I had to do. I had to call this thing off. I owed it to myself and to my kids to make a clean break from Steve before I began to even think about a new man, a new "white" man at that.

My inner critic was singing loud into my left ear. The date was a disaster, you would be doing him a favor if you called him and told him you can't see him again. Let the pressure fall off of him. Give him a chance to stop this thing without hurting your feelings.

Who was I kidding? Harvey probably would be glad to be let off the hook. So I picked up my phone and called Harvey. As soon as he picked up, I launched into the many reasons I could not see him again. I began with "I'm black, you're white, and we are both married." I ended with how I couldn't begin a relationship until I finished things with Steve, the importance of my kids, and making sure everything was taken care of. After five minutes of nonstop reasons, I paused and took a breath. Then I thought I heard Harvey say something strange. In fact, it was so strange I dumbly said "What? What did you say?"

He repeated it again and that time I heard it, but I had no reply.

Harvey calmly said, "I'll wait." I was so shocked at what I had heard that all I could say was "Okay," and then I hung up. What did that mean? I sat there at my desk thinking about it. I could hear people walking and talking in the background. Regular office murmurs, copies being made, phones ringing. Did I really hear him say that? I began to go over our conversation at lunch. He was clearly looking for relationship. I was interested in him, maybe too much and too soon. I could see his face as he was describing the woman that he was looking for. I could travel. I could hike. Well I could learn how to hike, its just walking, right? There were not too many places to learn this in Detroit. I knew nothing about any of the things he described but I knew I could learn. But *waiting*? Harvey was willing to wait for me to get my affairs in order. Nobody had ever been willing to do that for me.

So I sat there thinking. How long will he wait? He had already gone out with my friend. What if he found someone else while he was waiting? Something was telling me that this might be my best opportunity to have a happy relationship. In the few seconds that these thoughts flashed through my mind, I started panicking. What the heck was wrong with me? I picked up the phone and called Harvey again. When he answered I said, "You don't have to wait." I told him I was ready. We talked a bit more and then I calmed down. I no longer felt panicky or desperate. It was hard for me to believe that Harvey wanted to be with me as much as I wanted to be with him.

I got to know a lot about Harvey, including how he had once had it all and then lost everything. Although we came from different backgrounds, we found much in common.

It was hard for me to imagine that my children would decide against moving to Lansing with me. After all of the crying and discussion, they did not want to move with me. I understood that they wanted Steve and I to stay together. It was hard telling them that we would not be together. Even though we were very dysfunctional, Steve and I were the only family that they knew or had. My kids loved us both, but I was the problem. They saw me do too much. They experienced both of us at our worst, but they mostly believed that I was to blame—proven by the fact that I was breaking up the only family they knew. I explained to them that it was our chance to get out of Detroit, out of the ghetto. I tried to make them see that Steve and I could no longer be together because of everything we had been through. I felt like I had lived in a different house for seventeen years. Maybe they had not witnessed the same fights and beatings that I had. Maybe I dreamed it all. I began to waver in my decision to leave. Maybe I had it all wrong.

Then I remembered something that Harvey said; just the day before, he had reminded me that leaving Detroit was not going to be the most popular decision. "Don't think that it will necessarily go over smoothly with your family." In my children's eyes I was the problem and now I was trying to move them and split up their family. They were right but I was also trying to move them to someplace safe. The days leading up to my move were hard. I was not sure if any of my children would go with me. In the end, they all decided to stay in Detroit. Tamiko rented a flat for herself, Aaron, and Michaell. It was even harder once I told them about Harvey. The kids never openly said anything about him being white. It was more that with him in the picture, it was less likely that Steve and I would get back together.

It was 1999. I had almost six years sober and I was heartbroken. What had it all been for? Then I remembered that I had to do this for me; I could not continue to live for anyone else. I again heard my daddy's voice: *you ain't never gone have nothing because you give it all to those kids*. I love my kids dearly but I was also learning to love myself. I hoped that my children would eventually come to see that.

I visited Daddy right before I moved. His health was failing. By then, his alcoholism had begun to manifest itself in other ways. His body had begun to break down. Daddy had suffered from diabetes for a while, but we knew it would not be long when we found out he had been diagnosed with cancer. Because I was changing, I was able to make peace with my daddy. I remember him telling me that he was proud of his children. He told me that he was most proud of me because I had managed to do something that was extremely hard. I had stopped drinking. I know he said this because he struggled with the same problem. In the end, he became grateful for little things, like being able to sneak away from Ms. Mary and walk to the pizza parlor for a diet forbidden cheese slice. Harvey was there for me during those sad times. My dad died of heart problems, cancer, and a whole host of complications from alcoholism.

Harvey told me what he learned through the years about loss. He told me that he deals with difficult times by making spaghetti. Sometimes when you don't know what to do, a simple act can get you out of yourself. Over the years, I learned that when I'm feeling sad, angry, or anxious, I clean. Most days you can tell how I'm feeling by how clean my house is.

When Daddy died, Deborah took on the brunt of the responsibility and made all of the arrangements. Deborah put aside her resentments from the past and laid our father to rest. The funeral was hard.

Ms. Mary kept saying that she was determined not to be a statistic: the remaining spouse dying within six months of their long-term partner. I took Harvey over to Ms. Mary's house shortly after the funeral. I wanted her to meet him, and I wanted her to know that I was happy. Standing on the small porch, I rang the doorbell. I heard her at the top of the stairs. She could see us through the small window in the door. "Is that you, Brenda?" I said it was. "Is that white man with you?" We sat inside and talked for quite a while. We still laugh about that today. We lost Ms. Mary five months after Daddy. I like to think of Mama, Daddy, and Ms. Mary in heaven looking down proudly at me.

In Lansing I learned a lot about myself; though these insights did not happen quickly. I realized that I was important. I realized that my God loved me and I was slowly becoming who God had always wanted me to become. I was learning how to be a good person. I had someone in my life who believed in me and who invested in me.

I remember when it dawned on me that in this relationship I was waiting for the other shoe to drop. I was excited and afraid all at the same time. I wondered whether my relationship with Harvey could handle an argument, or the possible return of my kids. I did not want my dream life to implode, leaving me truly all alone. It took a lot of time for my kids to forgive me. Once they saw that I loved them no matter what, they started visiting me in Lansing. We all began to experience many firsts.

One "first" was a Mother's Day Brunch at a swanky, top-notch hotel. There was a buffet and it was very dressy. I remember Michaell being excited when she saw the ice sculpture of a dolphin that had champagne flowing down into stacked glasses. Harvey was good at showing the kids how to treat me. He arranged the entire brunch, paid for it, and then told me that it was from the kids. Harvey would take them out to shop for my Mother's Day, birthday, and Christmas gifts. I always knew that it was from him, but what he was doing was showing them how to treasure me as a mother. I really respected and loved that about him.

Another "first" happened during a particular visit from Michaell and Tamiko when we decided to drive around Lansing. They both wanted to explore. They questioned me, wanting to know where the bad part of town was. Lansing looked so different from Detroit. There were no rundown houses, none that were burned out or boarded up. As we drove around, we could not find a single neighborhood that was likely to be termed "a ghetto." On another visit, I took them to the local swimming pool and we talked about how they felt. I talked with them about how I felt and why the divorce was good for Steve and me. I told them how the move to Lansing was what I felt I needed to stay whole.

That first Christmas with Harvey and my kids was the best. Harvey gave everybody a piece of paper and told us to pick three things that we wanted. We also started a new tradition: everybody would buy a Christmas ornament and place it on the tree when we decorated it. Years later, I find it still moves me when I pull these ornaments out of storage. We also started a night of open-me-first gifts. When I told friends or coworkers about this practice, it was as if I had just discovered the most wonderful thing. Most of my coworkers already had this tradition, but I had not even heard of opening a gift on Christmas Eve and wearing new pajamas for the holiday. How special and brand new we all felt about such a little thing. I've learned that the best thank you to yourself could just be buying a brand-new pair of underwear. Nothing feels as good as a new pair of panties on your booty. New Christmas jammies felt the same.

When Harvey and I moved to a house on Sawgrass Street in a gated community, he casually handed me the key as he left for an out of town business trip. I was busting with excitement about living in a newly-built home. I would be the first one to cook there and to sleep in the new house. When we had first discovered the house, I felt apprehensive just driving around the place. I just knew security would see us (me) and kick us out for trespassing. Harvey got out of the car and started for a house that was not completely built yet. While I sat in the car, he disappeared inside. I was shitting bricks waiting for the cops to pull up. I just knew that some nosy neighbor would see me sitting in the car alone and would know that I was up to no good. I was afraid of my own breath back in those days. Harvey came out through the garage and told me to come inside to take a look. I was afraid to move for fear of getting in trouble. I had never been in an unfinished house. I didn't have to put on an act with Harvey. He knew that this was totally new to me and that it was blowing my mind. I felt that with Harvey I could go anywhere. I had instant access.

At work with my new house key in my hand, I was busting with the news. I had to tell someone about it before my head exploded. I did not have anyone to call, who I thought would be happy for me. I felt like my family would see it as bragging. So I told my coworker, Elaine. I was beaming with joy. I was so excited that I drove her to my new house on our lunch break. As I drove through the gate and put my key in the door, I knew that this feeling would last a lifetime. We tentatively walked around inside, but soon enough we became like little schoolgirls. Running through the house, we screamed about the newness of it all; Elaine grabbed me and hugged me, telling me how happy she was for me.

It was a pivotal moment. I ended up telling her my feelings about being apprehensive about my kids not coming to Lansing with me about how the whole idea was for me to move them out of the ghetto and into a better neighborhood. I told her how it broke my heart that they did not want to come. I told her how bad I felt that I was divorcing their father and tearing their home apart. And then I looked at her and I said, "Do you think I'm doing the wrong thing for my kids and me?" She looked at me, looked at the house and then she told me that what I was doing was the best thing for my kids.

The first snow that fell after we moved to the Sawgrass home was beautiful. Because the subdivision was still being completed, there were many lots with wonderful, untouched snow. Harvey had a set of snowshoes and he was determined to show me how to use them. I never played too much in the snow when I was little. I never played too much with my kids in the snow either. It was always one reason or another: not liking being hit by snowballs, not wanting Tamiko to get sick. Mostly though, I just didn't like the cold. This snowfall was different though; it was magical. After breakfast Harvey and I walked out into the quiet, white landscape to the empty lots full of fresh snow. He showed me how to put the snowshoes on and captured the moment with his camera. I felt that all was right with the world. As soon as he took my photo, I tried to walk and fell backwards in the snow. I was so bundled up that I could not move and Harvey had to help me get up.

At some point, Harvey decided that we needed a vacation. I had never done anything like that. Our first vacation was to the Bahamas. Of course I needed a bathing suit, so off we went to Somerset Mall, the most expensive shopping center in the suburbs of Detroit. Eventually I would come to love getting dressed up to go shopping like the other shoppers. But loving the experience of that fancy mall was something that had to grow on me.

I remember the first time he took me there. We were living in the Lansing apartment and he asked me if I had ever been to a ballet. Of course I told him that I had not. But like most little girls, I used to dream of being a ballerina. I believe it was our one-year anniversary as a couple and he wanted to celebrate. Dinner and the ballet: but first I needed a little black dress.

I immediately felt that I did not belong at the mall. I was angry with Harvey, and at myself for letting him talk me into going. I had on blue jeans and gym shoes, which is what I normally wore on the weekends. I felt that everyone was looking at me because of my casual attire, and because Harvey and I stuck out like a sore thumb. I felt ashamed, and Harvey was oblivious to it all. We passed stores that I had only ever heard about. I tried to steer him into Macy's or something like Forever 21. But no, into Neiman Marcus we went. I was shocked at the prices; I could buy four dresses for what one of those cost.

Harvey seemed to be enjoying himself. He picked out dresses for me to try on. Alone in the dressing room, the bad talk between my ears was so loud I knew I had to focus on getting through this experience. *They ain't better than you and you ain't better than them*, I reminded myself. After viewing them all on me as I paraded out of the dressing room, Harvey asked me to choose the dress that I liked best. I chose the least expensive one. After we bought the dress and some matching shoes, we had a bite to eat it at P.F. Chang's. I was introduced to lettuce wraps. I could not wait to bring the kids here to try them.

There were many moments like the Somerset Mall incident where I felt out of place. Most of the time just being with Harvey helped me get through. But sometimes I had to give myself a good talking to. I had to ask myself why I didn't think I belonged. I began acting as if I did belong. Faking it. Holding my head up and saying to myself, *yeah look at me...yes I'm here and so what?* Inside the privacy of my own head, I used my militant black voice: *You can't make me leave and you better not touch me.* Most of the blatant racism Harvey and I suffered came from black people in Detroit.

There were many good times in the Lansing house, so many "firsts," and our relationship was solid. I got all dolled up in my new little black dress and we drove from Lansing back to Detroit. We had dinner at The Whitney. It was wonderful, I felt so special. As we were leaving the restaurant Harvey asked me what I liked most about the ballet. I really loved the costumes and the music, but what I liked most was the men's packages. I remarked that I thought they must really have socks stuffed in their tights for the packages to look so big.

Harvey's response was, "You know, I think I'm going to marry you." I took that as a proposal. It became a running joke with us: did he or didn't he ask me to marry him?

Harvey wanted to do so much for the kids and me. He wanted us to be safe and happy. Most of the things Harvey did were directly because of his love for me. He realized that Tamiko was having a hard time getting to work so he went to Detroit and bought her a used car. When she needed a place to stay, he put money down on a flat; when we found out that it was located in an unsafe neighborhood, he put money down on an apartment. Aaron moved in for a while so he could attend the better high school in Lansing; Harvey got him a used car. Michaell came and lived with us for a while; to make her comfortable, Harvey bought her a color television. He hosted a party to celebrate Aaron's graduation from high school and my Bachelor's degree.

When Aaron wanted to have his own apartment, we contracted the same company that built our house to renovate the basement. But we got over our heads on the deal. When it was almost completed, we could not afford the upgrades and we had to sell the house. Harvey was devastated. This was the first argument Harvey and I ever had. It wasn't about whose fault it was that we were losing the house; we argued because we felt differently about the move. Harvey felt like a failure. Though I wasn't happy that we had to move out of our beautiful home, I wanted to look on the bright side; at least we could afford to go someplace else. It was not like all our stuff would be set outside on the street.

This was when I discovered how different we were culturally. I told Harvey that I knew how to live poor. It didn't matter to me if we live in a gated home, I just wanted to live with him. I had lived in poverty before and could go back to it if need be. I knew how to survive in harsh circumstances. That set the foundation for our financial relationship.

There were many times when I felt that Harvey was all I had. He was with me when Mike was going downhill. I asked Harvey to go with me to Detroit to try one last time to talk to Mike about trying sobriety. Mike welcomed me in with a hug. I could tell he had been drinking, but he was coherent. The first thing Mike said to Harvey was, "You know, I really don't like white people." I was a bit stunned. But Harvey, being a straight talker, said it was okay; he didn't like some of them himself. Mike told me that he was not an alcoholic because he only drankbeer. So I hugged my brother and after a while we left. Sometimes I would wake up in the middle of the night after having a bad dream about him and I would call Mike to make sure he was okay. Then I enlisted Tamiko, Michaell, and Aaron to bring him to Lansing for the holidays. He came for two Christmases before his drinking got so bad that the kids were afraid to bring him. Not long after that, I got a phone call from Deborah telling me that Mike was dead. He had been drinking, and either had another stroke or had just blacked out. He hit his head on an end table when he fell and was lying there for three days before anybody found him.

There was the brother who saved me, who took care of me when my daddy and everyone else left. Michael worked hard for years to take care of me, and now he was gone. I tried to understand it; I still try to understand it today. Mike had been strong for both of us at such a young age. We were both just thrown out into the world and did the best that we could. Then once we both got on our feet a little, we both fell victim to alcohol. I found help and he didn't.

This is how grace works, I guess. In some ways I felt like it was my fault. I found help, but I could not save him from alcoholism like he had saved me from homelessness and abandonment. Over the years, I've learned that I don't have the power to decide who gets saved and who does not. I can only carry the message. I loved Mike dearly. He was able to hold on long enough after Mama died. I believe he would have made it, but alcohol just brought back the memories of loss and made him sicker and sicker.

I have carried an unhealthy fear of Detroit that is still with me to this day. When I look back on it, I can't believe I actually lived through those times. I'm afraid of that city because I've seen the horrors.

After we lost the house, I got the idea that I should be moving up in my job since I had earned my security certifications and my bachelor's degree. I had also started an MBA program, so I started looking for a better job. The state of Michigan had been my only employer for seventeen years. It was where I had learned how to work. I had gone from being a clerical worker, to a security specialist, to being the only woman certified in information security in the State of Michigan. I thought I had arrived. However, when the opportunity to move up came, I was not ready for it and I missed my chance. A new security chief had been hired and he met with me because he had heard that I was certified in security. The certification was so new that, even as the director, he was not certified. He respected me for having this certification. This was the first time I felt valued at work; I had something that they respected and envied. When he gave me the option to pick whatever job I wanted in the impending reorganization of the security department, I faltered. I'd never been offered such an open-ended choice. Asking for time to think about this, being indecisive in the moment, proved to be my downfall. I lost the opportunity. Once again, I found myself at the top of my pay scale with nowhere I could advance to within the system.

I began to send out resumes all over Michigan in search of a new job. Months went by with no job offers. Harvey suggested I look outside Michigan. He had supported my getting the certification even though I had to take off work for two months, take money out of my 401(k) to pay for it, and drive daily back to the outskirts of Detroit for the training. He suggested I get the MBA, and he supported me when I did not think I was good enough to do it. When I have had fears about anything, Harvey has always been my beacon. He believes in me. So I thought about what he suggested, though I could hardly imagine it. I was both scared and excited. Yes, I had moved to Lansing from Detroit, but this would be bigger, I felt it.

Follow the path, my higher power would whisper. This path felt right. Now that I was on this journey, the path seemed to open up and it flowed before me. I just had to keep doing what was in front of me.

As a salesman, Harvey could work from any state. So I asked him where he would like to live. He told me we probably couldn't afford to live in California or New York. Harvey suggested that avoid offers for a position in Texas, Arkansas, Alabama, Mississippi, Louisiana, Florida, Georgia, or the Carolinas because we are an interracial couple. He said he liked Colorado, but that his favorite place was the Seattle, Washington area. Thus, I began my online, nationwide job hunt.

But I was more than unsure; I was terrified. *What if I succeeded?* Because I was so afraid, I became my own best negotiator. When I talked to recruiters, I often asked for a lot of perks and definitely pushed the boundaries. I researched the top salary for each job and I always asked for a bit more. I asked for signing bonuses, relocation costs, vacation time perks, stock options, everything I could think of. I figured not too many people would want me to give what I had been asking. When they were willing, I somehow managed to find something wrong with the job. I was sabotaging myself. I would complain if I didn't see a lot of women or black people in the office, or I didn't like the atmosphere.

Finally, I interviewed for a position at a bank in Ohio. There was this awesome feeling of becoming. They met every one of my requests. I was interviewed by each of the four vice presidents in one day. Everyone, including the bank's hiring manager and the VP that I would be working under, assured me that I had the job.

The recruiter had showed me around the city and we even picked out temporary housing until Harvey and I decided where we wanted to settle. I was to come back in a few days to meet and be interviewed by the VP and Chief Information Officer, which they all assured, was a formality. When I met with him, the CIO acknowledged that I was more than qualified for the job. He then asked me if I had decided what part of town I wanted to relocate to. I told him the name of the city that my husband and I had chosen. There comes a time in every interview when I can tell whether or not I have the job. Up until that point, I knew I had the job. But the CIO looked at me, perplexed. He said, "You can't live there. That's where I live." I knew that this guy was being prejudiced and I knew that I could either let it slide or I could push. I decided right then to push, because at this point it was a matter of pride.

I said to him in a sweet, professional voice, "If you are happy living there, what is it about the area that you think I would not like?" At that moment, I saw the job float away. He said that he thought there were many other cities nearby that would suit me better. We both knew that the deal was over. We were just trying to finish it. I stood up and we shook hands. As we did so, we both silently acknowledged that he was a racist and that was the end of that.

I kept in touch with the recruiter and one of the VPs. They were astounded at the outcome. Even though I appeared strong in the interview, I sank to the floor at home and cried like a baby. *Was this the way that it would be out here?* Then I had second thoughts and I prayed. Eventually, I realized that the bank job was not for me. I began to understand that I was shown the truth about the CIO before I was stuck in the job. I was so glad that it had happened that way.

Not long after that I got an offer from a utility company in Ohio. I was on my way, making the big bucks. I was the top breadwinner in the family. Harvey would kid me about this, saying that he could get used to being a kept man. Soon I was approved to buy a house. My God, how far I had come from trying to stay ahead of the landlord! I tried to remain humble, still afraid, but trusting my higher power more and more each day. Once I stepped out there I began to experience more faith. Faith is like taking your car to a new mechanic. He fixes it for you the first time and does not charge you a lot of money; you will come back the second time. If he fixes it the second time you are more likely to recommend him to your friends who are having the same problem.

The job in Ohio was different. I felt that it was my chance to do real security work. Harvey and I found a large, wonderful house in the town of Pickerington. I was still holding out hope that my children would want to move in. Instead, we had a dog to keep me company when Harvey would go on his business trips. Cindy was a yellow lab with issues. She would chew through doors when we left her alone. We loved her dearly.

Shortly after I began working there, the company started cleaning house. The reorganization would manifest with a hit list of managers who were being released from their current position. The list would be released every Friday. "Black Friday," as it was known, made this a very depressing place to work. I got scared and decided I would be proactive. I re-opened my resume on Monster.com and was contacted almost immediately by the recruiter at retailer in Seattle. I remember driving from Detroit to Ohio after visiting the kids, when I got the call from the recruiter. Six months at the utility and I was ready for the really big move to a new state hundreds of miles away from Michigan.

I knew a little bit about Seattle, having visited in late winter several years before. At that time, it rained every day that I was there. Harvey was excited. We had not talked much about this possibility. His favorite words to me were, "We don't have to make a decision on moving until they offer you the job." At this point, we were still in the interview stage. I had received the interview travel information via email from the HR recruiter. I liked him immediately.

The retailer would fly me into Seattle, and put me up at the Grand Hyatt Hotel in downtown Seattle. Fancy, smancy. I was being courted. There were a few problems. I was not a seasoned traveler at all. My flight was delayed; by the time I got to Seattle, I was tired and cranky. I had no time before the interview to go to the hotel. I had to change into my interview suit in the ladies' room at the airport. Dragging my luggage with me, I walked into the building on 7th Ave., not sure if I would be alert enough to answer any technical questions during the interview. By this time, Michaell was pregnant with my first grandchild back in Detroit. The baby decided to come right as I was being interviewed for the job. I was hoping to call Harvey to check on Michaell's labor. Harvey still worked in Michigan and had greater access to the kids. He and Tamiko went to the hospital with Michaell.

When I got to the interview, the first thing I noticed was how laid back everyone was. All except one woman were dressed casually.

One guy in the interview even had a face piercing in the middle of his eyebrows. This was a bit distracting. It was a typical interview. I could tell that they had made up their minds to hire me and that this was just a formality. They started trying to convince me to take the job. They listed various reasons and I must have looked uninterested. The head of the security group asked me if I thought I wanted the job. I told him that my daughter was in labor and that I was worried about her. "I could live here," I told him. "But right now I just want to leave to call and check on my baby girl." Of course, they understood. The HR recruiter got me onto the next flight out of Seattle and flew me straight to Detroit.

I had to wait to get the red-eye flight, so I had a little time for a meal. I walked down to the waterfront. It was July 2005 and Seattle was experiencing a bit of a heat wave and it was brightly sunny. It was nothing like my previous visit. I stopped at a seafood restaurant and had a bite to eat. Harvey called me to update me on Michaell. He said that she was having trouble, and that while delivering the baby, she had asphyxiated on the operating table. The doctors thought they had it under control and Harvey assured me that the baby was doing well. Harvey put Michaell on the phone. I told her that I would be on the next flight out. As I sat there crying and feeling guilty for not being with my baby, I glanced out of the window. Just then I felt something. I looked, and all at once Mt. Rainer came into view. It was the biggest, most beautiful thing I had ever seen. In that moment, as I stared with my mouth wide open, I realized that God was there with me. This mountain was proof of what He could do. I told Michaell that I knew that she and the baby would be okay. I knew it in my soul because I had just seen a miracle. I made it to Detroit in time to hold my brand new grandson.

We decided because she had had such a hard time, that Michaell and the baby would come back to Ohio with me to recover for a few days. She is a very strong woman, by far, stronger than I am. Jaylin was born with a few problems, like an allergy to formula. That first year was very trying for her and for Tamiko, who helped out a great deal during that time.

I accepted the job in Seattle and began my transition to retail. Between 2004 and 2005 my income increased by forty grand a year. This was hard to fathom. Ohio was just a dress rehearsal, a place to learn how to be away from family and friends. I did not know it at the time, but it was more like a test run on how to get used to being with myself. Seattle was full of new things to see; I was constantly calling Harvey to tell him what I had witnessed.

One day, I saw a flatbed truck with a gorilla in the back playing a piano! Another time, I saw a man dressed as a giant penis and the dykes on bikes ride by; it was the gay pride parade. I remember calling Harvey to tell him how strange it was to not feel like salesclerks were following me when I shopped, and that I paid someone with a check and they did not ask me for two pieces of identification.

One time when I was feeling depressed about being alone, felt I had made the wrong decision and had been banished to a faraway land, I saw a beautiful hummingbird flying around a rhododendron bush in the middle of February. The weather and seasons were different; flowers bloomed in February and March. What a life I had been given. I was making huge adjustments from what had become familiar in the suburbs of Michigan, to what was ordinary in Seattle. The thread of continuity in my life between these two places was that I spent much of my free time working on my program of recovery and hanging out with fellow recovering folks who also enjoyed a life of sobriety.

I spent a lot of time exploring the city. Not going too far but taking small baby steps. I went on a bus tour to Mt. Rainier. What a huge mountain! I remembered my miracle with Michaell and Jaylin. I went to the Chinese Gardens and to many museums.

I had taken a job that I had little experience in. The position called for me to create a Security Awareness and Training Program. I was to train the executives and employees with the new program. The funny thing was that I did not like speaking in front of people. I used self-help books, journaling, and morning mantras to help build my confidence.

After conquering my fear of public speaking, training over five hundred employees in my new job, watching the department I worked in dwindle, and feeling like I merely fulfilled a box to check off on the company audit form, I knew I had to move on. This was the second becoming. I could either grow or stagnate. Right when I thought that I could not take it anymore at my job, one of my co-workers showed me a posting for a position up north in Bothell at Cingular Wireless. Six months later I began working there in a new job with even higher pay. I was their one-woman IT Risk Management team, doing real security work at last. I loved it. Within two months, Cingular became AT&T and I got to work on the next greatest thing before anyone even knew of its coming: the iPhone.

Harvey would work three weeks in Michigan and then stay in Washington for a week. Then, it shifted to two and two, and eventually he moved out here fulltime. When he would visit, we would go house hunting. We met a very nice realtor on Bainbridge Island. She and I became fast friends, and we remain friends to this day. Harvey fell in love with Bainbridge Island and really wanted to live there, but at the time I thought that this was out of our budget range. The housing market was a sellers' market. Each house for sale ended up in a bidding war. I was not used to this. They were small houses starting at half a million dollars. And to top it off, we still had houses in Michigan and Ohio to sell. We really had high-class problems. Eventually, we were able to do some creative financing, and Harvey and I bought a house on the island.

Around this time, I was walking around Pioneer Square in old downtown Seattle thinking about what we were going to do. As I was walking, I heard rushing water. I followed the sound and discovered a manmade waterfall right in the heart of the city. It was a cool place. I sat and thought about my life. I meditated and relaxed. Finally, I ended up back at the museum that had bigger-than-life paintings. I just wanted to step inside and become a part of the scene. That's when it hit me: *I belong here. I have become who I am. I live on an island. How did I get here from where I started?* Just six short years before, I had been living in squalor, with sewage flooding my basement. My mind said, *Brenda, you don't belong here.* But again, I didn't listen.

That voice has gotten weaker; fear does not hold me in its grips. I am the strong one now. I have courage and I have integrity. Each day I never forget where I came from, but each day I'm so excited about where I'm going.

HARVEY'S MAKING SPAGHETTI

O n every business trip back to Detroit, Harvey would check in on the kids. Often, he would have dinner with them to see how they were doing. One particular time he was there, Tamiko got sick and went into a sickle cell crisis. She had been living with Michaell, helping out with Jaylin. She was also working fulltime and going to school. Tamiko was putting a high strain on herself, trying to do too much. She had always been able to bounce back after one of these crises, but the last few came quicker and lasted longer. Harvey decided that it would be a good idea for Tamiko to move out here with us. This had worked well for Aaron who moved to Bainbridge soon after he got out of the army. He had spent two and half years in the war and we were glad to offer Aaron free rent and a chance to get his life together. It was hard for Tamiko to leave her Dad, Michaell, and Jaylin, but even she had to admit that the crises were taking more of a toll. I agreed, because I knew that the medical treatment here in Washington would be much better than in Michigan.

Tamiko did well here. I tried to get her to just kick back and take it easy, but she needed to feel useful. She found a new doctor and was being treated at the Seattle Cancer Care Alliance. She found a job and was even able to take classes and graduate from the community college. One day while riding the ferry, Tamiko met and fell in love with a man who would become her husband. We had a wonderful wedding in Sequim and a great reception in Bremerton. Living here, Tamiko had gone a couple of years without any major crisis. Tamiko and her husband moved into an apartment less than an hour away from us and she seemed to be doing well.

Then, it seemed to come from out of nowhere. She got really sick. We were told to prepare for the worst. The hospital did not know what was causing so many of her problems. It seem that the sickle cell had begun to affect her vital organs. Her kidneys, liver, and heart were being impacted. There were many times, while writing this book, that I was not sure if Tamiko would make it. I prayed to God and, for the first time in a long time, I cursed at him, too. *How*, I wanted to know, *could you allow my baby to go through so much pain? Either take her, or leave her the fuck alone!,* I would scream.

Harvey made spaghetti and I kept the house clean. Harvey and I talked to palliative care doctors and nurses. No one could tell us what the prognosis was. Eventually, the only thing they could offer her were strong drugs to hold back the pain. At some point, I decided that I could not sit around waiting for my daughter to die. I had to continue to live. I was not helping her by not taking care of myself.

ONE STEP, ONE BREATH, ONE HEARTBEAT

I remember when I first saw Rainier, The Mountain. It seemed so close yet it was from far away. Seattle is some hundred miles away from the mountain and on this particular day, it was out. The people here say that a lot, "the Mountain is out." It's like when it rains they take it somewhere to store it, wait until the sun comes out, and then they roll out Rainier to showcase how beautiful it is.

Seeing Rainier for the first time took my breath away. It became my stabilizing point whenever I need to be reassured that God was all-powerful. Rainier gave me strength to continue out here in Seattle alone, waiting for Harvey to move here with me. Waiting for my life to start, waiting for love to return, waiting for my kids to forgive me. Rainier waited with me.

Eventually, all of my beautiful island life started showing up around my waistline and the next thing I knew I could barely keep up with Harvey on our hikes to places like Hurricane Ridge and the hikes around Mt. Baker. I could not even walk the trail on Paradise on Mt. Rainier without huffing and puffing. I was so out of shape that I was glad when he decided to go on an eight-day trip across the Olympic Wilderness alone. I bought a GPS SPOT tracker and a medic bracelet for him and sent him on his way. When I picked him up, he was so fulfilled and peaceful. I could see a change in him. His eyes told most of the story.

After looking at his photos, I decided that I wanted to be able to share this with him. I wanted to go on these long types of hikes. I remembered that this was part of our deal. He had wanted someone to hike with him. So I started going to our local gym. I mean really going. I had been a member at the gym for a year or so, but I was not going on a regular basis. So I decided to hit it hard. I signed up for their Train to Lose program. It was regular exercise, nutrition help, and accountability check-ins. The pounds and inches soon came off. My confidence soared. After training regularly for six months at my gym and losing weight, learning how to eat right and changing my lifestyle, I begin to see that I could have progress. I had faith that I could keep this going and I also recognized that I was a person who needed a goal to keep the weight off.

Although I had fleeting thoughts about the possibility of climbing Rainier, these thoughts were always in the back of my mind, too crazy to share with the rest of the world. The gym gave me the opportunity to entertain these thoughts with others.

The Train to Climb program was structured around exercise, strength building, and nutrition with the end goal of climbing Rainier. Nine months of slowly building my body and mind. Taking me from a person who was fit due to weight loss and transforming me into an athlete.

I would get strong enough to mountain climb. I found that I needed a goal to continue the exercise. I needed to be accountable to someone for my progress. Harvey was skeptical at first, having tried to climb Mt. Rainier twice before and not making it to the first high-mountain stop, Camp Muir. Being a bit naïve, and buoyed by my success with the other program, I said, "Why not? If I could lose weight and work the TTL program, I could follow the TTC program too." I could climb Mt. Rainier.

The program was hard. We worked our way up in weight and distance in increments. We did training in the gym, with hikes in the Olympics and Cascades. We climbed every mountain on the Kitsap Peninsula. I had one problem; I was slow. I could hike long distances but I had a problem keeping up with the group. I also fell a few times. Soon, though I was training on Mt. Walker every weekend. This mountain is 2,804 feet high with an elevation gain of 2000 feet in two miles. This translates into a very steep climb. It was during one of these beginning climbs that I injured my leg. This injury was from training too hard and too fast with too much weight. I did not start slow as the trainer suggested. I wanted to see how much weight I could carry so I began with forty pounds in my pack. Finally, I started listen to my trainer, but the damage had been done. Then one rainy morning I slipped on Walker and fell. I thought that would put me out, but somehow I kept going.

The next training mountain was an overnight climb up Mt. Adams, 12,280 feet. This was the big test. I climbed Adams shortly after I had been injured. My doctor from the sports clinic told me all I had to do was get up the mountain. My problem was that it was painful climbing down. He told me that medicine like cortisone would not last long enough for me, and to just focus on going up. "Climb down backwards if you have to." That's the kind of people who are out here in the Pacific Northwest. Of course, he had climbed Mt. Rainier like so many others who grew up living in the shadow of the mountain.

On Mt. Adams I made it up 9,400 feet to the overnight spot of Lunch Counter, where we got rained and snowed on. The next morning I was determined to not try to summit because the weather was too bad. I quit the program that night and a few times after. The self-doubt was constant. *Who do you think you are?* Or worse: *Who are you trying to be?* Old voices of self that I had not heard for years came back to haunt me. I almost quit after Mt. Adams; I had so much pain. I was slow going up and in pain coming down.

It was hard, but I was invested. I spent six days in the gym and hiked on the seventh. Somewhere in the front of my mind, I knew that I could do it. Somewhere in the back of my mind I was being told different. I think what pushed me on was what has always driven me. My lifelong question to myself: *Why not? Why not me? I should be able to climb this mountain; others have.* My prayer life increased and I got closer to God with every hike. Every time I fell down, every time I pulled out, I prayed for help. I prayed to God to give me a graceful exit. I prayed for strength to continue and for the good sense to stop. Just when I thought it was over, I would get the strength to continue. The hardest times were when the training had ended and there was nothing left but to climb the mountain. I was in the best shape of my life, though I was still slow. Most people had counted me out, or so I thought. *Never mind,* I said to myself. *I paid my money for this, so let's go to the bitter end.* Harvey was supportive, as always, but I could tell that he was worried about me. On July 25, 2013 Harvey drove me to Alpine Ascents on Queen Anne to begin the three-day adventure. I did not get much sleep the night before, as I spent hours packing and repacking my backpack. Trying to make sure that I had what I needed and removing things I didn't. I went over that climb a million times in my head. *I could do this,* I told myself.

We arrived and went through the gear check. All of that meticulous packing was undone as we reviewed what I had. Then we all drove to Paradise Lodge at Mt. Rainer to meet up with our guides. As we were gathered there, I cried because my brain had begun to count me out. It was too late to back out, so just like that we began the climb. This was a feat that no one I knew had ever accomplished. Harvey told me stories about how he and Pat O'Leary had tried twice and could not make it past the Muir snow field. I was determined that even if I was slow I would make it to Camp Muir. That alone would be an accomplishment. At the start, this was all that I was hoping for. The day was very sunny and warm, above average for the mountain. I started out with too many clothes on, so by the time we made it up to the trailhead I needed to remove a few layers. The 45-pound backpack was heavy and it felt as if, because of the winter hiking boots,

that I was dragging at least twenty pounds on my feet. I had a GPS tracker attached to the top of my pack so that Harvey, the kids, and anybody else could watch the climb on a computer or mobile device. I began to worry about this also.

There comes a time in every hike or climb, if you are pushing yourself past your known limit, you cross over into a different zone. This zone is where I am torn away from what I believe I can do and realize that I am doing something else, something that I have never done. Here in this place is the spirit. Here is courage but there is pride also. I was proud of myself for giving this a shot. This is also the moment when I always ask, "Whose freaking idea was this? Who talked me into this?" Then I always realize that I am the culprit and that the only recourse is to finish it.

Slugging along slower than the team and being watched closely by the Alpine Ascents guide, I made it across the steep snow field and up to Camp Muir (10,188 feet), where I collapsed into my rope buddy's arms. It had taken the team five hours to make it to Camp Muir. It took me six and a half. So exhausted but exhilarated too, I did my standard yoga pose like I had done at the end of so many grueling hikes. This triangle pose had become my mark of competition. I was glad that it was over. I made it to Camp Muir and I was content with being higher than I had ever been. This contentment was lost on the Train to Climb lead, Michael.

When I made it to Camp Muir, I felt that the journey had been worth it. On the previous training hike to Muir, I could not even make it that far. But this time, when it mattered, I did. As I fell into my spot for the night and got into a ball in my sleeping bag, I knew that this was it. I felt good. I was now farther up this mountain than anyone I knew.

Michael had a bit more faith in me than I did. Convinced that after a night's rest, the next leg of the hike to Ingram Flats would be a piece of cake, Michael convinced me to continue on. While it was flatter, the air and the backpack worked against me as I again slowly slipped behind my team.

What drove me on? In the beginning of training, Harvey told me that I would need a mantra to repeat to myself as I climbed. This mantra could be a piece of poetry, a song, or a prayer. This is what I would count on to get me up this mountain when all else fails. Something to repeat to give me strength to push on. My massage therapist gave me hers, "One Step, One Breath, One Heartbeat." When I thought I could not move up the mountain, I repeated the mantra.

Once I made it to Ingram flats I felt that it might be possible, after a few hours sleep, to make it to the summit. The crazy realization set in that *wow, I just might do this thing.* As a group, it was decided to forgo the sleep and continue to the summit so that the climb could coincide with the sunset. The team voted to continue so they could see the sunset. I was the only one who voted to wait until we had a few hours sleep. So off we went.

Even with a lighter pack, I knew as soon as we started that I didn't have enough stamina to summit. But something kept driving me on. Before my legs started giving out, I made it up to the aptly named Disappointment Cleaver. So close to Little Tahoma, the second highest mountain in Washington, that I could almost touch it. Up in the clouds, closer to God than I had ever been. The day was clear, crisp, and beautiful. At times I could see clear to the Sound. At other times I could see Mt. Baker, Mt. Adams, and Mt. St. Helens. This was the greatest feeling I had ever felt. My legs began to buckle and I knew that this was when I would stop. As the team continued to the summit, I knew I had gone as far as I would go. This spot was my climax, my summit.

My guide and I sat down and marveled at how far I had come. We sat and celebrated my climb by eating all of the candy that was designated for the summit. I could see so far off in the horizon. I was up in the clouds. I thought of how proud my mother and father would be of me. I was proud of myself. This was a great accomplishment.

Going down was the best. I always loved going down because this was where I got to lift my head up and see all of the sights that I had not able to see when I was focused on the struggle to get up the mountain. Here I noticed the wildflowers and the birds and marmots along the trail. Here I reveled in the fact that I was now a mountain climber. Pat O'Leary would later tell me that I had earned my ice ax. That meant so much to me. Harvey was waiting for me as I arrived dirty, tired, and happy. The first thing he said to me was, "So what are you going to do next?" Just like that I started thinking about my new goal.

It took time for the shock of what I had done to wear off, for the reality to sink in. It was nice to see all of the support I got from my family and from my friends in the community. I wanted to do something next that was a bit less stressful. I was naive in selecting my next adventure. I wanted to do more of a trek than a summit of a mountain. After reviewing colorful brochures of the trips that were offered by Alpine Ascents, I chose the trek to Everest Base Camp.

With the help of my Island Fitness trainers, I began another program to train for the trek. Kathmandu, Mt. Everest base camp. A reason to keep training. I trained for six months before I began the next adventure. Harvey drove me to Victoria, B.C. where I flew first to Hong Kong then to Kathmandu. Here I would begin the 22-day trek across Nepal. What a shock this was. Such beautiful, friendly people. Sights, sounds, and smells, I never imagined. The air was heavy with incense and everyone was dressed in beautiful colors.

At first I thought the difficulty I felt in my chest was the smog, but I eventually realized that my past suicide attempt and surgery had resulted in a diminished lung capacity. While my mantra to get up Mt. Rainier had been "One step, One breath, One heartbeat," here it became an old prayer that I remembered as a kid. For this trek, I would need to go straight to the Big Man himself if I was to come back alive. I repeated this prayer to get me through: *He's my rock, my sword, my shield. He's my wheel in the middle of the wheel. I know He can and I know He will, fight my battle if I just keep still.*

God gave me a Sherpa named Nema who stayed with me through the trek. Nema was patient, kind, and spoke very little English. Nema became my savior. When I became too tired to go on, he drove me with these words: "Move, Brenda." There were times in my exhaustion when I wondered if I passed out would he carry me or would he stand over me yelling, "Move, Brenda."

We started out from Lukla (9000 ft.) and in ten days would end up at Everest base camp (17,598 feet). I would come close to breaking my body and mind, almost as close as my addiction had brought me. But there was an exhilaration in this also. Meeting a group of people who shared my love for being out here. Day after day, meeting the die-hard mountain climbers whose only reason to exist was to climb. There were forty people in my extended group. Some were trekking just like me, others were on their way to climb to the top of Everest, and then there was the true adventure seeker—the guy who would climb up to the top and then jump off in a bird suit.

Many times on this trip I wanted my mother, Harvey, the kids: anybody to hold me and tell me that I would be okay. On the seventh day of this trip I surpassed 13,000 feet, higher than Mt. Adams, or

Rainier. On the day that we reached Everest, I had taken many pills to combat the symptoms of altitude sickness. This resulted in my hands becoming numb.

The day started out warm so I did not pack my rain/snow pants and I did not have on my snow goggles. We arrived ahead of the group, having been sent out first because I was slow. We celebrated with photos and the standard yoga pose. When the team arrived, our leader took one look at me and decided that I should get back to the teahouse. As Nema and I returned, we ran into a blizzard. Nema guided me through, taking time to wipe the snot from my face before it froze, as my hands could not perform this task. I was in bed delirious for two days after that, but I would not trade that feeling of standing on Mt. Everest for anything. I was standing on the top of the world. Me. A little black girl from Detroit. When I made it back to the U.S., Tamiko was still in the hospital.

EPILOGUE

"I'm glad I don't look like what I've been
through." Bishop Richard White

There are times when I look back on my life and I think *why
didn't He give up on me?* Why was I given a second chance? I
think about all of the people that are now gone. Dorethea, the
friend who helped me see that there was another way out. She told me
that other people did not drink to solve their problems, but she ended
up a victim of crack and—when the tables were reversed—I could not
help her out. Those loved ones who helped me to become the woman
I am. My mother, Mike, Daddy and Ms. Mary. How different would
my life have been if they were here just a little longer?

My sister and I have recently spent some time together talking about
our childhood. I remember being so happy, but she remembers other
times. Times when she was so hungry that she stole Mike's baby food.
We both wonder what happened to make our father leave Mama, and
we both are dealing with life on life's terms.

Tamiko has gone through a long and difficult illness. I can't imagine
the pain of sickle cell anemia. She has endured this pain since she was
old enough to breathe. There comes a tipping point for both of us with
this. I was back from my trip and Tamiko was in the hospital. This
was nothing new. What was new was the length of time she had begun
to stay. This last time was a six-month stay. It was as if she lived there.
The pain was being somewhat controlled, but there did not seem to be
an end in sight. Finally, after some intervention with hospice she was
sent home with a pain pump attached to her intravenously, and in that

173

instant, I moved from chief advocate mother to chief advocate mother and primary caregiver. My life revolved around Tamiko.

Before being discharged, there were many times we thought she was at the end of her life. Her abdomen was so swollen from liver dysfunction. Her body would swell, and overnight she would balloon up in weight from 106 pounds to 126 pounds. It was maddening. The damage spread to her heart from water in her lungs. She screamed out in pain almost daily. The toll this took on me was not evident until Tamiko was home, stable, off the pain pump, and doing somewhat better.

My climb to Rainier had spurred others to become interested. I agreed to go on a practice climb on Rainier with a friend with the goal of going as far as we could—maybe to end at Camp Muir. I knew something was wrong. I had been having swelling in both hands, and after this climb I was in so much pain I had Harvey take me to the emergency room.

I knew I had Rheumatoid Arthritis (RA) having already researched my symptoms on the Internet. I tried not to think about my prospects for the future but I admit I was scared. I also knew that, ultimately, God would take care of me no matter what.

While writing this book, there were many mornings that I could not write or type. At its worst I could not wash, dress myself, or even perform basic things like toilet tissue usage on my behind. It took months before I was scheduled to see a specialist, then I was put on a regimen of drugs that were more damaging to my body than the RA was. Harvey's spaghetti pot got a bit bigger.

I had to hang up my Tamiko chief advocate hat and become my own advocate. How long could I work? Would I need to move to a house that was more accommodating? How would I finish this book? Talk-to-type programs became my best friend. God always makes a way. Sure I got depressed, but I had my community of recovery and my family to help me through. Just as I was getting relief from my pain, Tamiko was also diagnosed with RA. Together we have both struggled through the side effects, and twists and turns of the medical system.

My doctor told me when I first saw him, writhing in pain, that he would have me hiking in six months. Slowly my RA went into remission, only to return again and again. I kept up with the yoga, and one day after I had convinced Harvey to remove his biases about Hawaii and take a hiking trip there, my yoga instructor called me and asked if I wanted to go to Spain to hike the Camino. I casually told her that I needed to talk to Harvey about it, not thinking it would be a problem.

I got up to go into the bedroom and, as I passed the mirror, I had to do a double take. *Who are you* the face seemed to be asking. *Here you are trying to decide whether to go to Hawaii or to Spain. What kind of life are you leading? What kind of friends do you have that call up out of the blue and invite you to Spain?*

In six months, I was in Spain walking with thirteen other women. We walked the same path that many pilgrims had trudged before us. Although I had some flare ups, I was able to walk 120 miles of northern Spain. I am still amazed at the journeys I have traveled and will continue to travel.

My life is much different from the way I dreamed it would be. As I lay in my neighbor's yard or sat high in the apple tree, I only wanted a small house, two children, and a husband who loved me. I got so much more than that. I got better than I deserve. God gave me grace and mercy, and I accept both wholeheartedly. I am proof that you can get here, from there, if you just have faith and follow the path.

CPSIA information can be obtained
at www.ICGtesting.com
Printed in the USA
LVOW10s0035110517
534091LV00001B/149/P